Available soon:

For more information visit our web site

www.oup.co.uk/vsi

Penelope Wilson

HIEROGLYPHS

A Very Short Introduction

OXFORD
UNIVERSITY PRESS

OXFORD
UNIVERSITY PRESS

Great Clarendon Street, Oxford OX2 6DP

Oxford University Press is a department of the University of Oxford.
It furthers the University's objective of excellence in research, scholarship,
and education by publishing worldwide in

Oxford New York

Auckland Bangkok Buenos Aires Cape Town Chennai
Dar es Salaam Delhi Hong Kong Istanbul Karachi Kolkata
Kuala Lumpur Madrid Melbourne Mexico City Mumbai Nairobi
São Paulo Shanghai Taipei Tokyo Toronto

Oxford is a registered trade mark of Oxford University Press
in the UK and in certain other countries

Published in the United States
by Oxford University Press Inc., New York

British Library Cataloguing in Publication Data
Data available

Library of Congress Cataloging in Publication Data
Data available
ISBN 0-19-280502-9

1 3 5 7 9 10 8 6 4 2

Contents

Acknowledgements

I would like to thank George Miller at OUP for first approaching me to write this book and Emily Jolliffe for helping me through the process. I was lucky enough to be taught by Professor 'Peter' Shore and some of the discussions here stem directly from him, though some years ago now. I was especially glad to track down the Nekau II scarab discussed in Chapter 7 as I remembered it as a Christmas homework exercise from my first year at university. It has taken until now for me to realize how interesting it was. I would like to thank Roger Dickinson, Wendy Kinder, Karen Exell, Don Wilson, and anonymous readers for reading the text and improving its readability in numerous ways.

The book is a somewhat personal account based on material I have read or studied. Any omissions are a result of my own limitations and the opinions and any errors in it are my own.

This book is For Roger *r nḥḥ ḏt*

List of illustrations

Chapter 1

The origins of writing
in Egypt

Setting the scene

The civilization of Ancient Egypt existed between around 3500 BC
and 30 BC. It occupied the area of the valley and delta of the River
Nile northward from its First Cataract in the north-east corner of
Africa. With desert to the west, east, and south and sea to the north
and further east, the Nile Valley delineated the Egyptian state. It
was also incredibly rich in all kinds of resources including abundant
fish, birds, wild and domesticated animals, many varieties of stone
in the desert quarries, and metals, especially gold, in the eastern
wastelands. Most importantly there was a flood which revitalized
the agricultural lands every year with fresh mud.

The people of Egypt have left behind monuments and objects, many
of them covered in the writing now known as Egyptian hieroglyphs.
They used this pictorial sign system to write down their language
and record aspects of their culture. The information from the
writing tells us something about how the Egyptians governed their
land and people, about their beliefs, and about their hopes and
dreams. Though we can read hieroglyphs this does not mean that
we know everything there is to know about Ancient Egypt, partly
because the writings have survived accidentally and so are a fraction
of the original corpus and partly because the writings only preserve
those things the Egyptians themselves thought were important.

This means we have to tread a very careful path in interpreting and attempting to understand the writings, for our sources are biased by chance and by design. They do, however, give us a point of contact with the minds of the Ancient Egyptians.

Ancient Egyptian is classed by linguists as an Afro-Asiatic language. This means that it is related to North African languages such as Berber and Cushitic, and to Asiatic (or Semitic) languages such as Arabic and Hebrew. Modern Egyptians speak Egyptian Arabic, not Ancient Egyptian, which is now a 'dead' language. The ancient language was a mixture of words connected by a grammatical system spoken by people in the north of Africa and the Near East.

Early rock pictures

The earliest people who lived in the Nile Valley may have originated in different places, each bringing with them different aspects of language and vocabulary. One such area was the savannah-like region on the edges of the Sahara bordering Egypt on the west. The people living here around 5000 BC were hunter-gatherers and cattle herders who depended on the food they gathered and their animals for their existence. They would have needed to remember good grazing areas, water holes and routes across the waste margins. Such memories would be passed down orally and possibly also in pictures.

Rock pictures left behind by these early hunters are found in the Western Desert in the areas of the Gilf Kebir, Uweinat, and around the Kharga Oasis.[1] These rock pictures may be the beginnings of pictorial writing in this area – that is, the means of communicating a thought or idea by drawing a sign with a tool held in the hand. Although they are notoriously difficult to date, some of them are found in close proximity to Neolithic settlement areas and relate to the lifestyles of the people in this region. They also show the beginnings of the visualization of concepts and the need to formulate a common means of communication in some way. These two ideas of communication and visualizing images are the central concepts in understanding writing and Egyptian hieroglyphs.

The earliest rock-art images show the things which were most important to those who drew them. They show different groups of people with different lifestyles. At Uweinat the cattle breeders drew mostly cattle and showed themselves leaping over them and herding them with their crooked staffs. They also hunted ostriches with their bows and arrows. In the Kharga Oasis area were men with head-dresses, hunting animals, including antelopes, giraffes, and wild bulls. The people of the more mountainous areas in the east hunted rhinoceros, elephant, and ostrich. The images were either picked out of the rocky outcrops in the desert with stone picks or were painted in red or yellow ochre, black charcoal, or gypsum. The animals no longer exist in these parts of the world because it is now too dry, but clearly at this time, around the end of the fifth millennium BC, they were important to the hunters.[2] It is possible that the hunters drew the images either before the hunt as a wish for what they would catch or after the hunt to record what they had captured. Some of the scenes may have been accompanied by oral stories and acted as illustrations for the hunter as he regaled his companions with his exploits. In such cases the pictures act as cartoon images representing frozen actions, but they also show the cognitive link between pictures, words, and sounds.

Clearly people were drawing pictures of things important to them at this time, but they may have written on other things now lost to us, such as animal hides, shells, plant leaves or bark, and even themselves. They could have covered their bodies with painted designs, tattoos, and perhaps also pictures of important things, such as the ostrich they wanted to catch the next day, or the bull whose qualities they wanted to acquire. These images and pictures enable the process of sympathetic magic to work and this is another key concept in the use of writing in Ancient Egypt.

Boats, landscapes, and people

As the savannah areas dried up through climate change, the raging torrent of the River Nile became calmer, allowing people to move into the Nile Valley and delta and begin to live off its fish and water birds and to cultivate the muddy fields of its flood-plain. Rock drawings of boats may relate to the first contacts between the hunters of the savannah and the riverine and marsh people of the Nile Valley. In old water courses called wadis in the Eastern Desert of Egypt, there are also many rock drawings of which the earliest also relate to the boat people.

The boats vary in shape – some have flat bottoms and right-angled keels while others have rounded bottoms. The boats usually contain people and oarsmen, although sometimes they contain standards and animals which may relate to early gods or chiefs in the Nile Valley. The first Predynastic cultures in Egypt and in particular Naqada II culture in Upper Egypt (around 3500–3300 BC) also

1. Rock pictures including animals and a boat with deities or heroes. From site 26, Wadi Abu Wasil, Eastern Desert.

painted pictures of boats and desert landscapes on pottery vessels which were buried in tombs. There is no doubt that boats were important within the Nile Valley for transport, perhaps for warfare, for trade, and for the status of early chiefs (in the same way that limousines or yachts stand for millionaire status in our culture) and this may be the reason for their prominence. At certain times of year the wadis could have been covered in grass after rainfall and at this time expeditions may have been sent into them to collect semi-precious and hard stones or plants or to hunt desert game or to graze flocks and herds. The boat pictures could also have acted as reminders of home for the valley people or markers of the rank of individual expeditions sent there. It has long been suggested that they could also represent expeditions sent out to the Red Sea to go further afield and that they could even suggest actual contact with other riverine traders outside Egypt at this time, particularly with those from Mesopotamia. Some of the boat images in rock pictures and on pottery may represent mythical stories about heroes who ventured or came from beyond Egypt. The people of this area at this time may have been able to recognize the tale about the hero meeting the round-bottom boat people at sea, the story of the hero reaching a mystical island, the hero finding the fabulous black stone of the desert, or the hero making his epic journey across the desert back to his beloved valley.[3] All of the boat images may relate one story or they may tell a thousand different tales. It is impossible for us to know because we have lost the oral narrative, but something is being communicated here and its culmination is in Tomb 100 at Nekhen (Hierakonpolis).

Tomb 100 was the tomb of the chief of Nekhen, one of the early states of the Egyptian Kingdoms. The tomb consisted of a number of small chambers made of mud brick and was partly sunk into the desert surface. When it was discovered in 1896 it had been robbed out completely, but the paintings on its walls, though damaged, told a remarkable story. There were scenes showing a series of boats of all kinds with dancing women, desert landscapes, animals, animal hunters, the capture and slaying of human prisoners, and also the hero who tamed wild animals. The tomb has been dated on stylistic grounds and from the archaeological material associated with it to the Naqada IIc period, about 3300 BC. The scenes seem to be a culmination of all kinds of visual arts from Predynastic Egypt. Is the tomb a repository of the most important myth of the people of Nekhen or is it one man's life, shown with his family at certain important times – the first hunt, religious rituals, his death? It may be a narrative or an advertisement, a fantasy or an idealizing autobiography.[4]

Élite writing at Abydos

A little later at Abydos (the cemetery of another early kingdom at This), the local rulers were also being buried in élite tombs with separate compartments for the body of the dead chief and for the goods which were buried with him. The man buried in Tomb U-j around 3200 BC was very wealthy and his goods included jars of resin or wine from the area of Syria-Palestine, a dish made of obsidian, an ivory sceptre, and many other things of which only the labels have survived. Around 190 labels were found in the form of small rectangles of wood or ivory carved with pictorial hieroglyphic signs showing a variety of information. The most simple bore numbers: one vertical stroke represented one object, two strokes denoted two objects, tens were shown with an inverted horseshoe shape, and hundreds by a swirl. Each label had a hole bored in the corner so that it could be tied to whatever it denoted – perhaps a box or bag containing, for example, three (lengths of cloth), two (festival bread loaves). These numerical signs are the earliest recognizable writing from Egypt – a symbol specifically designed to give information which cannot otherwise be deduced. The single units would be clear but the swirls would have to be understood as numbers by both the writer and the viewer. A second group of labels show a variety of signs in a bewildering series of associated groups. They have been interpreted as representing goods from different places: a shrine resembling an elephant together with a real elephant may represent Nekhen or Aswan; the jackal perhaps stands for the jackal lands of Middle Egypt, while the archer may represent the tribes of archers in the Eastern Desert – perhaps those who sent bows or arrows as tribute to this powerful Abydos ruler. There are writings of the placenames Buto, 'Fighter-City', and 'Ship-City', the identities of which are otherwise lost. The most complex labels may show administrative activities such as bird hunting, fish catching, and cloth production which were directly controlled by the ruler's residence and harim. Altogether around fifty signs are attested, both signs with sound values only (*phonograms*) and signs with meaning values only (*semograms*), indicating the level of sophistication of writing at this time.[5]

Tombs dating from the Predynastic period often contain pottery vessels, probably not because the pottery itself was always intrinsically valuable but because of their contents – fats, unguents, ointments, perfumes, beer, wine, resin, grain, meat, pickles, preserved fruit, or dried meat. Pottery and stone vessels were the plastic boxes and bags of their time. Often these pots were incised or drawn in ink with a sign such as a circle, a pair of arms, or a cross and in these cases the signs do not describe the contents (no doubt labels were used, since jars could store many different items). These signs instead seem to indicate ownership – either of the pot or of the jar and its contents – for when the kingdoms of Egypt were united in the Early Dynastic Period, around 3100 BC, we find that these pot marks contain the names of the early kings of the country. They are written as a rectangular box called a *serekh*, half covered in a series of vertical lines with a picture sign in the other half and a falcon standing on top of the box. The falcon is a sign for the king, the box represents the royal residence and the sign inside the box is a writing in pictorial script of the name of the king. It seems logical that the most important things should have been among the first things to be identified by this writing. Here the king's name denotes his ownership of the jar and its contents. The *serekh* is a stylized representation of the palace complex with a niched-facade enclosure wall and is the first identifier of a king's name, at once protecting it and symbolizing the institution of the palace administration.

Commemoration and accounting, ownership and display

Writing in the tombs of the Early Dynastic Period at Abydos was used sparingly, so far as we can tell. This might, however, be a false impression. The tombs seem to be miniature versions of the houses of the kings and stored all his requirements for the next life. These ranged from food and clothing to oil for anointing (like aftershave and bath salts), plus exquisitely beautiful prestige and imported goods worthy of a king in the afterlife, so that his royal status was apparent to the gods. It was thought vital to record the ownership of these items so that there could be no doubt of it. It was also necessary to record the quantities and provenance of the goods so that the living would know how much had been placed in the tomb and therefore removed from the real storerooms of the palace. This suggests that the tomb records would then be compared with the palace magazine records and the two tallied so that the debits from the real stores could be accounted for. The royal stores no doubt comprised goods from all the king's domains and trading contacts and each of those places must have had its own accounts recording the taxes and tributes due to the king, what was actually paid and when it was sent to the residence. The tomb is the tip of the iceberg of a huge state organization and the use of writing in it hints at the huge accounting machinery at work in the background. It may seem less than glamorous to suggest that the invention of writing happened for taxation purposes, but whether material is recorded for the warehouse or for the afterlife, it is part of the same process.

The tomb too was a focus for the display of the cult practices surrounding the dead king and was not only the means for transferring him to another sphere of existence with the ancestor gods, but provided a restricted arena for the display of his power and status. In this sphere, the tomb architecture funnels life-restoring power to the king's spirit, whose existence is assured by the presence of hieroglyphs naming him.

Den (or Dewen) was one of the first great kings of Egypt, around 2800 BC. He ruled a united kingdom centred on the capital city at Ineb-Hedj, 'White Walls' (Memphis), and his tomb at Abydos is a good guide to how much written material might have been produced at that time.

At the entrance of the tomb were two monolithic stelae – inscribed stone slabs bearing only the name of the king. It was written inside the *serekh*-rectangle, with a falcon representing the god Horus standing upon it. Inside are the two hieroglyphs spelling the king's name: a human hand and a zig-zag water sign, Den. Inside the tomb many inscribed labels and jar sealings were found and they also record a second name of the king which is read either as Khasety or Semty. Some of the labels record 'events' or 'festivals' in the reign of the king and served as a yearly account (annal) of his rule. They record the kind of living myth that is the life of a successful king.

A close examination of one of Den's labels from Abydos shows how far the use of hieroglyphs and pictures had come up to this point.

2. **Label of Den from Abydos.**

The wooden label (British Museum 32.650) measures 8 cm by 5.4 cm and the text on it reads from right to left. At the top right of the label is the attaching hole and the tall vertical sign at the very right is a notched palm rib meaning 'year', so this reads, 'The Year of . . .'. The scene at the top right shows a figure seated on a stepped platform inside a booth. He wears a White Crown and holds a flail of office. In front of him a figure wearing the Double Crown of Upper and Lower Egypt and holding a flail and rod is running around two sets of hemispherical markers. The event is the Sed-festival, when the king proved his fitness and strength after a period of time in office by running around a marked course.

The scene below is less clear but seems to show a walled enclosure containing several hieroglyphs, perhaps the name of a town. To the left is what was originally interpreted as a small squatting figure of a woman with several hieroglyphs in front of her which may be her name. Behind her is a man wearing a head-dress and carrying an oar and a staff. Three hieroglyphs above him show a vessel with human legs, a bolt of cloth, and possibly a vulture sign. Behind him the two top signs spell the second name of Den and the lower sign is some sort of portable shrine. The damaged scene below contains bird, land, and plant hieroglyphs. The large area to the left contains the *serekh* bearing Den's name and to its left is a title, 'Seal bearer of the king of Lower Egypt', and the name 'Hemaka' (written with a twisted rope, a sickle, and a pair of arms). Hemaka was an important and powerful official of Den. To the left is another rectangle containing signs, of which the last one is a word meaning 'to build'. Beneath is a word meaning 'House of the King'. The hieroglyphs in the lower left part of the tablet can be recognized and mention the 'Horus Throne' and a dais. They seem to record further that the label was used on a jar of oil, perhaps recording its date of production or precise provenance. Alternatively, the oil may have been symbolically connected with the events depicted, either as anointing oil or offering oil. The tablet records 'The year of a Sed-festival, Opening the festival of the Beautiful Doorway', and perhaps something connected with the building of the king's palace.

As is clear from this part-interpretation, the signs have much information to give and act as a fully fledged writing system.

Altogether fragments of thirty-one such 'annal' labels are known from Den's tomb and they mention events such as the 'Journey of the *Reput* on the Lake' or 'Capture of the wild bull near Buto'. There is a clear tradition of recording events both with cultic and economic benefits. Other inscribed objects were found in Den's tomb including stelae with the names of people buried with the king, inscribed game pieces, and jar sealings. Some of them repeat 'cultic events' from the labels such as the Lower Egyptian king spearing a hippopotamus and, of course, record the name of the king. The most interesting personal object from Den's tomb was the lid of an ivory box inscribed to show that it had contained his own seal of office.[6]

There is also a hint that in cult temples the display of royal power was dependent on the integration of hieroglyphic writing and organized depictions of rituals or commemoration of events. The most famous example from this time is the Narmer Palette, apparently of Dynasty 0–1 (*c.*3100 BC) made of slate and decorated in raised relief. Found at Nekhen, it shows King Narmer, his name written with catfish and chisel hieroglyphs, as king of northern and southern Egyptian kingdoms. As the king of the southern Egyptian kingdom, probably centred on Nekhen, Narmer is about to brain his enemy, who is shown as culturally different. His death is not shown because the moment depicted is the precise second before the king acts – he can take life or give life. As the king of the northern Egyptian kingdom, perhaps centred on Nubt (Ombos), the king takes part in a victory parade surveying the decapitated bodies of his enemies and accompanied by a boy or man carrying his sandals and by a person wearing a heavy wig and leopard-skin garment. The figure is either his chief minister or a high-ranking priest. Though palettes were used to grind down pigments for use as bodily adornment, the size of this palette, its decoration, and the hieroglyphs on it suggest it was meant for display in processions or in the sanctuary of the temple to Horus at Nekhen. It commemorated the acts of Narmer and his devotion to the god Horus.

Materials

By the time of the Early Dynastic Period the principles of writing must have been firmly embedded in the system of kingship in Egypt for such a complex society to be able to run a cohesive administration. In this case, clearly, the writing and the ideas behind it came much earlier, but it is difficult for us to trace all the stages of its development. The painted Naqada pottery is hardly a full written document, but if such early documents were woven mats, papyrus, wooden boards, clay, or mud, they have not survived because they were not buried in the cemeteries whence much of the material has come.

The development of papyrus was also a crucial factor in the growth of writing as a means of communication. It is made from the reedy and abundant pith of the papyrus plant, which, when hammered together in thin strips and dried, forms a good, smooth writing surface which is easy to carry and could be rolled up and used several times. We know that the Egyptians were expert mat and basket weavers and so were used to working with all kinds of reeds and grasses from Neolithic times onwards. It is likely that they had experimented with making papyrus in the Predynastic period and with using it as a writing or painting surface for 'portable' messages. As can be seen from the early royal tombs, a vast range of writing surfaces were used: labels of bone, ivory, and wood on jars for incised inscriptions; jars for ink inscriptions; stone stelae inscribed with the king's name; flakes of stone painted with images (ostrakon). There are also mud seal impressions, again showing the ownership of various jars and their contents by the king. A roll of papyrus was found at Saqqara in the tomb of Hemaka, an official of Dynasty 1, but it was blank and unused.

Seal impressions are in themselves important as a means of easy replication of written signs, for one seal would be used to create a large number of impressions. Some of these early seals have survived in the form of a cylinder made of stone or wood. The 'cylinder seal' had a hole through the centre and the outside of the cylinder was incised in sunk relief with the writing, usually of the king's name or other words or a scene. When a string or stick was put through the hole it could be rolled over wet clay or mud and the impression of the seal would be left standing proud on the surface of the mud. Though this is a typical method of sealing jars in early Egypt, the cylinder seal was probably a Mesopotamian invention. The fact that the Egyptians adopted the cylinder seal has led to the suggestion that the idea of writing, and of writing in pictures (hieroglyphs) in particular, originated in Mesopotamia.

Mesopotamian influence?

Mesopotamia was the land between the two rivers of the Tigris and Euphrates, an area in modern Iraq. Around 3500 BC the Mesopotamian civilization based on the land of Sumer, with its capital Ur, was a powerful complex society with cities, a system of writing, and a fully developed administrative system to supervise tax collection and to manage surplus agricultural resources. It is likely that there was some kind of communication with the Nile Valley, perhaps by means of sea routes or by land routes giving access both to northern Egypt and through the wadi channels to Upper Egypt and the first main centres at Naqada, Nekhen, and possibly This. Mesopotamia may have needed raw materials such as gold, grain, or stone from Egypt, and Egypt may have wanted commodities such as tin and timber from Mesopotamia. There also seems to have been an exchange of invisible exports/imports such as technological ideas, cultural developments, and people. In Egypt it is possible to see some Mesopotamian technological and cultural traits during the Predynastic period and the beginning of the Early Dynastic Period: mud brick, niched facade architecture, subterranean houses (both at Maadi), and the 'man taming the beasts' artistic motif (Tomb 100). Among the ideas which came to Egypt could have been the idea of picture writing. In Mesopotamia, the Sumerian language was written in a pictorial script on clay tablets and carved on seals. Writing was used from around 3500 BC, particularly for documenting transactions and keeping accounts by the state administration. It may never be possible to tell from the archaeological evidence exactly how far Egypt was influenced by external factors, but if there had been contact, the Egyptians went on and developed their own writing system and its uses in their own way without drawing anything further from outside.

As more archaeological work is done in Egypt the evidence for the use of writing at earlier periods than is currently known may come to light. It also seems likely that any early contacts between Egypt and Mesopotamia will have left no real trace and that ultimately both civilizations developed their writing systems independently. Contacts between contenders are difficult if not impossible to determine but as both have similar geography and agricultural practices, it is no surprise that both would have the same requirements for the control of the state and its resources. It is interesting that in Mesopotamia the pictorial form of the script was dropped very early in favour of a much more efficient writing system using small wedge shapes called cuneiform. The Egyptians, meanwhile, developed a dual form of writing and kept the pictorial script for special purposes.

Stimulus and rule

In the case of Den's tomb, writing was used to name and identify, to keep accounts and to record specific cultic events pertaining to the king. The commemoration of these basic records achieved a cultic status of which the Early Dynastic tombs and Early Dynastic temple deposits are our only archaeological evidence. It is likely that they only refer to the rather rarefied élite sphere and record their concerns. The impression given is that in the valley and delta settlements writing was used more rarely for royal commemoration.

This cannot possibly be the case for every place, however, and the main administrative centres of Egypt will have had written documents of many types which have not survived. Indeed the success of the Egyptian state was based on the mass organization of agricultural surplus, so that it could be used to feed those who worked on non-agricultural projects for the king such as craftsmen, bureaucrats, the army, and members of quarry expeditions and the royal court.

The year's planning was based on one particular astronomical event. At the moment the flood began, the star Sirius was first visible from Egypt after a seventy-day absence. This coincidence signalled the beginning of the whole administrative year and it was all recorded. The timing of the rising of Sirius – the goddess Sopdet in Egypt – and especially the height of the flood were meticulously recorded and cross-checked. The flood began around mid-July, covered the Nile Valley and delta for about three months, and then receded. The ideal height was about 20 cubits (10 m) at Aswan, 12 cubits (6 m) near Cairo, and about 7 cubits in the delta (3.5 m). If this were exceeded settlements and farms could be destroyed, but if the flood fell short, not enough land would be flooded or water brought to produce the required food and surpluses. The southernmost part of Egypt at Aswan was therefore one of the key points in the country for measuring the flood height. As soon as the king's officials knew the height of the flood, they could calculate from their past records in the archives how much tax could be collected and therefore what kind of projects could be sustained for the glory of the king. This fiscal yield was broken down into units so that by the time the flood began to recede about three months later the scribes could be on hand to mark out the exact amount of land and inform farmers of their expected yields. From that first sign of the flood at Aswan a king would know what building projects he could afford, how many artisans and specialists he could usefully put to work, and perhaps how many foreign campaigns he could undertake. At times of low floods, the king would know that he needed to husband his resources wisely and perhaps scale down his building works and temple donations.

All of this was made possible by careful record-taking and accessible archives. Any king worth his salt would invest in his scribal training programme and he may even have come through it himself. Measuring, counting, calculating, and taxing were therefore the practical motivating reasons for developing a clear writing system in Egypt. The ideological reasons for the development of writing were concerned with recording this information to establish the status of the king in this life, in the next, and in the realm of the gods.

Chapter 2
Hieroglyphic script and Egyptian language

Sacred signs

Language is an evolving and constantly changing system. New words are created, old ones go out of use, meanings and pronunciations of words change, the structure of words alters, and the very grammatical framework of language evolves. The English word 'piggin', current in the sixteenth and seventeenth centuries to describe a small wooden pail or bucket, is now obscure, while the Old English word order with the verb last in a subordinate clause, as in 'they knew then that they naked were' has not survived. It was the same for Egyptian and both the spoken language and the script used to record it in the Early Dynastic phase had over three thousand years of development ahead of it.

The rise of the unified state in Egypt must have prompted development of a writing system to make accurate records for the benefit of the king and his court. Legend has it that the first king of Egypt, Menes 'The Founder', established the capital city at Memphis, at the apex of the delta, and that this was the administrative centre of the kingdom. It is no accident that the patron god of Memphis is the craftsman Ptah, who was believed to have created the world by thinking of the names of things. When he uttered those names, so giving form to thought, they came into existence. Writing is one of the ways of creating and recording ideas in a concrete form. The scribes and bureaucrats working at Memphis passed on their knowledge to their sons and laid the foundations for an élite class of literate bureaucrats. From the very beginning there was a difference between the hieroglyphic script and the cursive and linear hieratic scripts used in everyday life which would have been much more usual and more widely known.

The Egyptian word for their pictorial writing was 'medu-netjer', which means 'words of god', and it seems that this was recognized as the primary function of the hieroglyphic script: to communicate between Egyptians and their gods. This was possible in the buildings mainly associated with the gods, their temples, and in places where the divine world touched the earthly world – that is, in tombs and cemeteries. In addition, as the king was regarded as the intermediary between people and the gods, almost anything official or monumental relating to the king had to be written in hieroglyphic script. The drawing or carving of the pictorial hieroglyphs was a time-consuming process and if scribes had had to paint in every feather in every bird-sign it necessarily would have taken a great deal of time. Formal hieroglyphic writing was not a very efficient use of scribal time and so to speed up the writing process they had developed a shorthand script, which we call hieratic. The language written in this script is no different from that written in hieroglyphs and the scripts continue to be used in parallel with each other. It would be the difference between writing something in 'illuminated' letters like those in the Lindisfarne gospels or in Koranic calligraphy and writing something in 'real' (joined-up) writing. In general, the more monumental a text (temple, tomb, stela) then the more likely that it will be written in hieroglyphs. Egyptian is thus a dual creature in two ways: language and script; and hieroglyph and hieratic.

The Egyptian used in monuments had formal restrictions about how it sounded and was used, and particularly later on it must have sounded archaic and somewhat artificial. Whenever this kind of Egyptian was spoken or written it may have immediately implied a formal type of communication with the divine sphere (compare the different modes of address and degrees of formality in Japanese, which change depending on whether you are talking to children, for example, or to your boss). Monumental hieroglyphic Egyptian is an extremely high-status language.

Script

The scripts are usually written and read from right to left, but also occur reading from left to right, particularly for aesthetic purposes. The texts can also be written in horizontal lines or vertical lines. Egyptian is visually versatile and easily adapts to the place in which it is written. The presence of figural signs such as animals, birds, men, women, serpents, or fish and the fact they are usually drawn in profile means that they face one way or another. In order to make clear which way a text is to be read all these figural signs face the same way and the text is read into the faces of the signs. A single glance at a text is enough to see which way it is to be read:

In this example, the man with his upraised hands, the horned vipers, the quail chick, and the owl all face to the right. The text reads towards or into their faces (from head to tail) and therefore from right to left.

In Egyptian only consonantal sounds and not vowels are written, so that a basic written word could conceivably have had various permutations of vowel sounds attached to it. For example, the word for a house is written ⌂, p-r. It may have been pronounced 'per', 'aper', 'pero', or 'epre'. The pronunciation of the word might have changed depending on the function of the word within a sentence: 'the house is big' = 'per' (house is subject of the sentence); 'the man enters the house' = 'epre' (house is object of the sentence). By extension, nuances of tense may have been rendered in the spoken tongue but not in the written language, so they certainly existed but were not written.

In order to be able to communicate to each other how they understand Egyptian, Egyptologists use a system of converting hieroglyphs into a script based on the Roman alphabet. This method of rendering the characters of one language in those of another is called transliteration. For example, the word ⌒◉ is shown in transliteration as *rˁ*, the latter sign representing ˁayin, a sound not found in English, but which occurs in Semitic and in Arabic. It is pronounced something like 'raa' and is the word for the 'sun' or for a 'day'. When *rˁ* is written down, Egyptologists can therefore see how the word is being read and understood in the context of a sentence. For words which are spelled out this is not so vital, but sometimes words are written in a very abbreviated fashion and how they are understood could affect the meaning of a sentence. For example, ▭ by itself could be read as *pt*, 'sky,' or as *ḥry*, 'what is above' or 'chief'. With any luck the rest of the sentence in which this sign occurs (the context) will help to give its meaning.

Phonetic (sound) signs

There was not a true Egyptian 'alphabet' as we know it, but Egyptologists have devised an alphabet of a kind and this is used as a starting place in learning Egyptian hieroglyphs. The order of the signs is a modern, linguistic order and the list includes a number of sounds which are not heard in the pronunciation of the English language. It is very close to the claim of the Greek writer Plutarch that there were twenty-five consonants in Egyptian (*De Iside et Osiride*, section 56). All of the signs in this list are a single consonantal sound and they are written as if the text in which they occur is read from left to right.

At the beginning of the list are sounds which are classed as vowels in English but in Egyptian are consonants (basic element of speech). They are followed by sounds made with the lips (labial), palate, tongue, or throat and can be made with force or simply

sign	transliteration	identification	value
🦅	ꜣ	vulture	a (glottal stop preceding an **a**) aleph
𓇋	i	reed	i, y (Semitic yodh)
⌐	ꜥ	forearm	guttural unknown to english, ꜥayin a as in father
🐦	w	quail chick	w
𓃀	b	leg and foot	b
□	p	stool	p
🐍	j	horned viper	f
🦉	m	owl	m
〰〰	n	water	n
⬯	r	mouth	r
🔲	h	reed shelter	h, as in house
𓎛	ḥ	twisted fibres	emphatic h, as in ha!
⊘	ḫ	sieve	soft **ch**, as in Scottish 'loch'
⊸	ẖ	animal belly	hard **ch**, as in German 'ich'

21

sign	transliteration	identification	value
⚊ or |	s	door bolt/ folded cloth	s
▭	š	lake	**sh**
◿	ḳ	hill	emphatic k
▱	k	basket	k
🏺	g	pot stand	g
⌓	t	loaf or bread	t
⚬▭	ṯ	hobble	**tj** or **ch**
⬗	d	hand	d
⌇	ḏ	snake	**dj**

breathed. This is not a classification the Egyptians used. It is purely an artificial phonetic order for the convenience of modern students of the language and represents the monoconsonants (one sound) of the Egyptians. As Middle Egyptian has about seven hundred signs altogether and this list is of twenty-four signs it is obvious that the other signs used by the Egyptians represent other types of sound and also that they are used to represent ideas. Biconsonantal signs have two sounds, usually one of the above in combination with one of the first four sounds: ⚱ *mi*, 𓅯 *p3*, ○ *nw*, ⌒ *ḥʿ*. Triconsonantal signs have three sounds: 🪲 *ḫpr*, ♀ *ʿnḫ*, ✶ *zb3*.

Sound and meaning signs: ideograms

This group of signs are almost like real picture writing as they represent the thing they depict and have the relevant sound value:

22

⌐ *pr* house, 🜚 *ib* heart. A vertical stroke is written under such signs when used as a word to show that this is the case and that they are not purely sound signs.

Determinatives

Each word in Egyptian contains a number of these signs which can have different purposes in the word. The word for 'cat' can be written: 🜚🜚🜚🜚. The signs used to write this word are performing different roles within this one word. The first three signs are all phonetic signs to tell the reader how the word is pronounced. The first sign, a milk bottle with a string tied around it, is the biconsonantal *mi* recording two sounds and sounding something like 'mee'. The second sign, a reed, has the one-sound value *i* 'ee' and so adds to the *mi* and acts as a phonetic complement. The third sign, a quail chick, is another one-sound sign with the value *w* and the sound 'oo'. These three signs give the word the sounds 'mee-oo' and this is the onomatopoeic word for 'cat'. The fourth and final sign has a different role to play. This is an image of a seated cat, its tail curling up onto its back, as occurs in real life and in so many bronze statuettes of cats. The sign 'determines' the meaning of the whole word but it does not have a sound value. For nouns (the names of things), these determinatives are very useful in showing where one word ends and another begins, especially as Egyptian has no punctuation, except perhaps for the dots written above lines of New Kingdom poetry written in hieratic. For verbs (words which describe actions) there is another set of determinatives which reflect the type of action described. This can range from the obvious:

🜚🜚🜚 *wnm* to eat

🜚🜚🜚 *ḥwi* to hit

to the less clear:

🜚🜚🜚🜚 *s3* to be weak.

23

This word has a double determinative of a sparrow and a pustule. Both have 'bad' connotations in Egyptian. It is thought that the sparrow was used because it can convey the idea of 'smallness' or 'lack of something', so that although in itself it was not necessarily bad or threatening it could convey the idea of something undesirable. The pustule is a sign associated with disease and 'badness', but is not instantly recognizable and in fact there has been some debate over the identification of this sign.

> *rḫ* 'rech', to know

The determinative here is a piece of papyrus, rolled up and tied with string. As papyri contain writings and knowledge, the use of the determinative seems reasonably clear. This sign is a common determinative in words where it can be difficult to see the rationale for its use and it may in fact be used for much more abstract concepts. The determinative is therefore a kind of useful catch-all sign, as for example in *ḥr* 'her', be pleased, satisfied.

Determinatives have a much more important role than just being word endings for they affect the whole meaning of a word and can lend subtle (or not) extra meanings to words depending upon the context in which they are used. For example the word *wn* can undergo the following transformations by changing the determinative:

Meanings:

to be stripped off (of hair or branches), hairless

to hurry by (with running legs)

to open (with door-leaf)

light (with sun disk and rays of light)

child (with infant)

fault, blame (with sparrow, or sometimes with pustule sign)

Script and language: use and development

Egyptologists have divided the development of the language and scripts into stages. The current understanding of this development is dependent on the preservation of the material and the scholarly work undertaken so far. This means there are some gaps in our knowledge. Also, the rate of change in Egyptian was not constant and there is also some relationship with the type of text. Everyday texts such as letters or receipts demonstrate 'new' stages of the language earlier, whereas hieroglyphic temple and monumental texts show less variation but attain an archaic form.

Table 1 shows the way in which the scripts are used for certain types of text at certain times. These time frames do not always correspond to political changes in Egypt as shown in conventional chronological tables, but may reflect underlying cultural changes and reflect turning points in Egyptian society often masked by rigid king lists. From Table 1 it can be seen that these points of change are around 2200 BC and the change from Old to Middle Egyptian, around 2600 BC with the use of Late Middle Egyptian, around 1300 BC and the use of Late Egyptian, which in turn heralds the gradual move through Archaic Demotic to Demotic complete around 700 BC, and finally the use of Coptic probably from some time in the second century AD. The table does show that hieroglyphs were always in use in Pharaonic Egypt for its three-thousand-year history and that so long as monumental texts were required in temples to the old gods or tombs for the Egyptian religion, then hieroglyphs continued in use.

Stages of the language

Old Egyptian is the principal version of Egyptian used to write a group of texts in hieroglyphs called the Pyramid Texts. They were inscribed inside the pyramids of the kings and their queens from the reign of Unas in Dynasty 5 (*c.*2200 BC) onwards and are a set of spells, rituals, and descriptions of the route to the afterlife intended for use by the king. The idea was that the king could avert danger by

Table 1. Scripts and languages in use in Egypt

Script	3000 BC	2000	1000	0	AD 500
Hieroglyphs *Monumental & religious texts AD 495*	Abydos OE	Pyramid Texts ME Late ME	Archaic ME temples, stelae, statues, etc.	last text AD 495	
Linear Hieratic *Everyday texts* *Religious texts* *Monumental*		ME ME Coffin Texts: Late ME 'Books of the Dead' ME			
Cursive Hieratic *Everyday texts* *Literary texts*		ME letters etc. Late ME ME	Late ME LE		
Abnormal Hieratic *Everyday texts*			LE:Archaic Demotic		
Demotic *All text types (First Everyday, Last Monumental)*			Demotic		
Coptic *All text types*					Coptic

OE: *Old Egyptian*; ME: *Middle Egyptian*; LE: *Late Egyptian* the use of these texts, that he could communicate with the gods he would meet on his way to the next life and that he could gain extra powers and magical abilities using these texts. In addition, he would be able to make the transition from death to a life as a star and join with the imperishable circumpolar stars, the souls of the gods; he could become Osiris, the king of the afterlife; he could also be transfigured as light and serve the sun-god Re in his solar boat sailing across the sky each day. It can be argued that the texts cover a wider range of genres and imply a diverse origin from chants and hymns to narratives and poetry. It is thought that these texts represent a culmination of very ancient beliefs and ideas concerned with royal rituals about the identity of the king and his relationship with the gods. It was clearly felt that it was important to have a written version of the required spells so that the king would not forget them and so that he could have them for ready reference. For this reason they were carved into the walls of the king's burial chamber, beside his mummified body in its sarcophagus. At this stage the texts were not accompanied by any scenes or depictions of images and the signs were filled in with green or blue paint. The writings were probably composed by priests and wise men to form a compendium for use by the kings of the later part of the Old Kingdom. The Step Pyramid of Zoser and the great pyramids of Giza are largely uninscribed, so it is not known if these kings used earlier versions of the Pyramid Texts, perhaps written on papyrus and now lost. The texts became the basis for the more widely used religious spells known as the Coffin Texts (Middle Kingdom) and the Book of What is in the Underworld (New Kingdom and onwards).

It may be significant that the Palermo Stone was also written down in Dynasty 5. This is a remnant of a temple wall with royal annals like those from the labels of Dynasty 1. Something, perhaps political instability, occurred at this particular time to make the codification and collection of earlier writings a priority for kings. The impetus to collect, recopy, and edit texts over and over again is a practice which continued throughout Egyptian history and hints at the legitimizing power implicit in the hieroglyphic writings.[1]

Other documents were written in Old Egyptian. Autobiographical tomb inscriptions of officials, royal decrees, and a very few hieratic papyri containing letters have survived and there is also a famous set of temple archive documents called the Abusir Papyri. They must represent only a tiny fraction of a lost corpus of texts. The main difference between Old Egyptian and the later language forms is its verbal structure, with some inflected forms,[2] no pseudo-verbal construction at all.[3] So far as the writing of the language is concerned, the writing of the first-person suffix 'I' and 'me' or 'my' is often omitted and spellings of words are often cumbersome and full, with every sound carefully represented, sometimes more than once. In the Pyramid Texts there is a reluctance to split words if they go over from one vertical column to another, even to the extent of leaving a gap at the end of a column. In all there are about a thousand hieroglyphic signs known for this stage.[4]

Middle Egyptian was later regarded by the Egyptians themselves as the classic form of the Egyptian language and it is the most long-lived stage of Egyptian. It was used to write all kinds of texts in the Middle Kingdom and after that continued to be used to write monumental texts (in tombs and temples) until the end of the Ancient Egyptian culture. Spellings of words were standardized at this stage by the court schools, which meant a reduction in the number of hieroglyphs in use to around 750 signs. The hieroglyphic script was retained to write monumental and religious texts into the Ptolemaic and Roman periods, by which time over 7,000 separate signs were used. In grammatical terms both earlier stages of the language have a preference for the word order Verb–Subject–Object when verbs are used and this is known as a *synthetic* pattern. Here the verb carries all the information about its tense and mood in its own writing and all the information about the subject and object is attached to it afterwards.

Late Egyptian differs significantly from Middle Egyptian in its writing system, grammar, and vocabulary. There is a change towards a more roundabout writing of verb forms in which the subject is introduced by a particle or phrase which may also introduce tense and mood. The verb is then left to trail in second place. This *analytic* pattern therefore switches to the word order Subject–Verb–Object.

Middle Egyptian

sḏm = f verb (to hear, present tense) plus attached subject (he) 'he hears'

Late Egyptian

ir = f sḏm verb (to do), attached subject (he), actual action (to hear) 'he does hear'

The advantage of this system for Egyptologists is that in Middle Egyptian any subtle variations of tense were shown in speech by changes in sounds but did not show up in the writing. In Late Egyptian subtle changes in tense or meaning could be made by altering the introductory element and leaving the verb alone. This means that the writings for the sense, tense, and mood are converted but not the writing of the verb itself. This gives rise to forms such as:

i-ir = f sḏm 'that he hears'

wn = f ḥr sḏm 'he was hearing'

mtw = f sḏm 'and he will hear'

Note that in all cases the verb retains the same form in the writing and the same position in the sentence, but all the information about it is given by changing the first element.

Late Egyptian also contains foreign loan words, such as foreign city names, words for non-Egyptian things (compare in English 'sushi'), or which had come into common usage, like Egyptian *r-bl*, 'out' (compare in English *par excellence*). For example, one such borrowing from Semitic is the word for 'sea' 𓇋𓅓𓈗 *ym* 'yom'. This change reflects the increasingly cosmopolitan nature of Egyptian society, particularly in the capital Memphis from the beginning of the New Kingdom. The city must have been one of the great melting pots of culture and language in the ancient world and as the capital city of Egypt, the language spoken here drove the development of the language throughout the country. From the New Kingdom (if not earlier) there is a clear split between monumental texts written in Middle Egyptian hieroglyphs and documents and literary texts written in Late Egyptian, mostly in hieratic. In a sense, Middle Egyptian became an ossified language, like Latin as used in medieval Europe, while the Egyptian language itself continued to develop and change. Even Late Egyptian texts written in hieroglyphs look different, for example in the 'Hymn to the Aten' from Akhetaten. Many more smaller signs are squeezed together in word blocks and spaces are commonly filled with small vertical strokes or t-signs.

Late Egyptian itself was replaced in the seventh century BC by a 'new' script for writing the developed form of the language, both of which are known as Demotic. It is possible that the script was developed in Saïs, the capital of Egypt at the time, but it is more likely that the scribes of Memphis and Saïs worked together to develop this script for their mutual benefit and to put Egypt back on a stable footing after the invasions and rule of Nubian kings.

Demotic looks a lot less like hieroglyphs than anything written before and although ultimately it derives some of its forms from hieroglyphs, it is very cursive and is exclusively written from right to left. The language shows a continued development of the grammatical structures in Late Egyptian and the stage of Egyptian called 'Abnormal Hieratic' seems to be the link in the evolution of the language. In writing there is a marked tendency to use specific determinatives for verbs and others for nouns and the script is more methodical in writing plural forms of nouns using a plural marker.

It is used to write the same range of texts, however, including tales, prayers, letters, marriage contracts, shopping lists, oracles, and so on, all the rich material of ancient lives.

Demotic has a reputation for being difficult to learn and only a few people in the world can read it and translate extant Demotic texts. Some Demotic texts can be seen painstakingly inscribed on temples, funerary stelae, and official decrees. As the language in everyday use, it would have been heard in every market, on every street corner and in every home in Egypt. For most Egyptians at this time hieroglyphs were far removed from their daily lives. On the official Ptolemaic decrees recording temple donations, such as the Rosetta Stone or the Canopus Decree, the same text would be written in three different languages: Greek (for the ruling administration of the day), hieroglyphs (for the gods), and Demotic (for everyone else). The range of languages reflects the strata of Egyptian society at this time and the lines of communication. Demotic itself can be divided into chronological stages: early (Saite and Persian periods), Ptolemaic, and Roman, with the final datable text written around AD 450 in Philae Temple. The differences in the stages of Demotic can be seen in vocabulary, syntax (which could differ from one part of the country to another), and handwriting (which differed between individual scribes).

The final stage of the Egyptian language is first attested around the second century AD. At this time Egypt was part of the Roman Empire, which was slowly becoming Christianized. Coptic was used to spread the Christian message into Egypt and to translate Christian writings, mainly the New Testament and life of Christ, into the language spoken in Egypt. It seems, however, that 'Old Coptic' was created principally to write magical texts where the exact pronunciation of the words was all important. The language was effectively Demotic in a final form, but it was written in a different script and for the first time Egyptian was written in an alphabetic (uniconsonantal) script. From the second century AD Greek letters were used to write the Egyptian language, but because there were some sounds in Egyptian which did not occur in Greek, the scribes had to borrow a few signs from Demotic and use them along with the Greek alphabet.

ⲱ from , ϧ from , ⲍ from , ⲭ from , ⲋ from

This resulting script, the language and culture of Christian Egypt, is known as Coptic. Egyptian Christians or Copts make up one of the greatest religious and cultural minorities in modern Islamic Egypt and, in theory, Coptic is still spoken or at least used in the liturgy in the Coptic (Christian) churches of Egypt. It had died out as a spoken language by the sixteenth century. In AD 641 Egypt was invaded by the Arabs, who brought not only the religion of Islam but also the Arabic language. These largely replaced Christianity and Coptic. Coptic is valuable in studies of Ancient Egyptian because it can help in understanding some of the syntax and vocabulary of Egyptian, but more than anything else it is the nearest indication there is to the sound of Egyptian, preserving some of the words and perhaps the rhythm of the language.

The true pronunciation of Egyptian is still unknown, although much research has been carried out on this subject. No one living has ever heard Ancient Egyptian spoken, so though it can be read and understood, it cannot be pronounced properly. Coptic ⲏⲣⲡ, 'ee-rep', wine, suggests that this is how the ancient Egyptian word for wine sounded.

Equivalences:

	sn	ⲥⲟⲛ	'son'	brother
	itrw	ⲉⲓⲟⲟⲣ	'eye-oor'	river
	wn	ⲟⲩⲟⲉⲓⲛ	'wey-in'	light
	wˁb	ⲟⲩⲟⲡ	'wop'	to be pure
	wˁb	ⲟⲩⲏⲏⲃ	'weyeb'	priest
	wˁb	ⲟⲩⲁⲁⲃ	'waab'	to be pure/to be holy

Many words, often with a Christian connotation, were borrowed directly from Greek. The picture is also made a little more complex because Coptic preserves several dialects of Egyptian which were spoken in different regions of Egypt. It has to be recognized that this may reflect a situation in Ancient Egypt, where each region had its own way of pronouncing Egyptian and very possibly different grammatical idioms. Coptic occurs as Sahidic (Upper Egypt), Bohairic (Lower Egypt), Fayumic (Fayum area), and Akhmimic (a region in Upper Egypt) dialects and there may have been more. If it is difficult to discern local dialects in the surviving Egyptian texts, this may suggest that one of the rationales behind this rigid language was to provide an overarching language which could be understood throughout the country, particularly by the administration, while people also had their own versions of Egyptian.

Grammar

As in any language, there is a full range of grammar in Egyptian with rules about how sentences should be constructed. It has nouns (name words), adjectives (describing words, characterization), adverbs (giving additional information about actions), and verbs (doing words). The latter have tense (events in the past, present, or future), aspect (the kind of action, either completed or repeated), mood (indicative statements of fact, or subjunctive dependent on something else, or desirable), and voice (active action performed by subject, passive action performed on subject). The word order in Middle Egyptian is different from Western languages: verbs usually come at the beginning of sentences, 'goes out the man from his house'; adjectives come after the word they describe, 'He is a scribe, excellent, attentive'; sentences are made up of blocks of ideas in grammatical constructions: '*sun with moon* in sky' contains three basic ideas: (i) 'the sun and the moon'; (ii) what are they doing? 'in' and (iii) where? 'the sky'. The whole sentence then reads 'the sun and the moon are in the sky'. Egyptian does not have words for 'the' or 'a'

33

(definite and indefinite articles) until Late Egyptian and in many sentences not even for 'is' and 'are'. The fact that Egyptian seems to use markers, such as special words (particles) or constructions (word order) which act like my asterisks above to indicate when certain ideas are in operation or converters to highlight the differences in sentence meaning, is a major conceptual difference between English and Egyptian.

Other areas of language such as emphasis seem to be important in Egyptian and are expressed in other ways in English. For example, the sentence 'he goes to his house' naturally throws a certain degree of emphasis onto the subject 'he' by the very fact that 'he' comes first in the sentence. In Egyptian, the normal word order is for the verb to come first and so, in order to emphasize something other than the verb, various ruses, or grammatical forms, are used. Thus, we have the equivalents of the following, depending on what aspect is most important in the context of the action or story:

'HE goes to his house'
'GOES he to his house'
'TO HIS HOUSE goes he'.

This may seem like a small point but in the context of some Egyptian texts such as hymns, prayers, and literature, which have complex symbolism and ideology, every nuance is important and the various subtleties of grammar changing emphasis or tense are vital to our understanding. It should suggest to the student of the Egyptian language right from the beginning that ideas about language, how it is used, and how it sounds will be different from in European spoken and written languages. In learning Egyptian one is learning a different way of thinking, a different form of expression, and a different background culture. Rather than being a daunting process, this should make the challenge of learning Egyptian more exciting and give much more of an insight into past minds, thought, processes and lives.

The stages in attacking an Egyptian sentence are thus:

(i)   explaining how the phrase is written: from left to right, with honorific transposition of the first sign, meaning 'king', because it is considered to be the most important of all the signs

(ii) transliteration : *ḥtp di nsw* (putting into individual words, along the lines of pronunciation)

(iii) explaining how the phrase is built up (grammar and syntax): a relative clause

(iv) translation : 'a gift which the king gives'

(v)   understanding the phrase: one of the most common phrases on Egyptian funerary monuments; it refers to the benefits and gifts permitted by the king for the tomb owner or dead person

(vi) understanding the phrase in the context of the whole sentence: what will follow is a list of the gods of the cemetery who also allow gifts for the dead; then the list of gifts, usually along the lines of 'athousand bread, beer, oxen, fowl, cloth, ointment, alabaster, and all things good and pure'.

Imitators

Other ancient cultures tried to copy Egyptian hieroglyphs, in particular the kingdom of Meroe whose capital city of the same name was situated to the south of Egypt in the ancient kingdom of Nubia (modern Sudan). The kings of Meroe may have been descended from the Napatan kings of Dynasty 25 who had once ruled Egypt and regarded themselves almost as the guarantors of Egyptian kingship and as the protectors of the Egyptian gods with their impressive cult temple to Amun at Gebel Barkal. The Meroitic kings wrote their language in a form of pictorial script as well as in a more cursive script, like hieratic. It seems as if they borrowed the idea of the script from the Egyptians but, of course, they were writing a completely different language whose origins lay probably in ancient Nubian or one of the African languages spoken in

Eastern Africa in ancient times. Meroitic hieroglyphs form an 'alphabet' of twenty-four letters and, though the texts read from right to left, the animal and human signs face the other way.

3. Meroitic hieroglyphs. This text from an offering table is now in Berlin Museum, but originally from the Pyramids at Meroe. Eighteen of the twenty-four signs can be seen here.

Transliteration (reading right to left)	**Translation**
woshi : shore	O Isis and Osiris !
tekidje-mni qo wi	the blessed Takidje-amane,
npt-djxet : t edjxelo wi	born of Napata-djakhete,
	begotten of [Adjeckhetali]

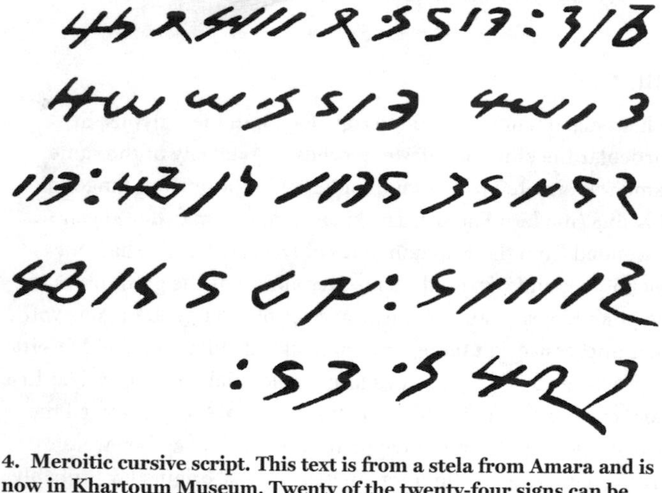

4. Meroitic cursive script. This text is from a stela from Amara and is now in Khartoum Museum. Twenty of the twenty-four signs can be seen here.

Transliteration (reading right to left)	Translation
woshi qetene yinele	O Isis, (epithet)
shore qeterre	O Osiris (epithet)
adjemeqo le wi : qo-	Adjemeqo, born of
-koye : djxelo	Qekaye, begotten of
mni-teme	Amani-teme

Few of the signs have the same appearance as the Egyptian
hieroglyphs and none has the same value. In addition, Meroitic uses
punctuation marks, a kind of colon between words, because there
are no determinatives. The texts normally read from right to left
and the cursive form is easy to recognize as the signs look like rows
of numbers 2, 4, and 3, some of them with very long tails. Though
the basic value of the alphabet is understood, the Meroitic language
is still not totally deciphered. The basic meanings of some funerary
texts can be understood, but the detailed meaning of long historical
accounts is much less clear. As scholars continue to work on the
language there may be a breakthrough like the recent work done on
Mayan. What is needed, however, is some kind of bilingual text,
perhaps written in Meroitic and Demotic or Meroitic and Greek, so
that the same two texts can be compared and understood. One of
the last surviving sites where that might have been possible was the
sacred hill site of Qasr Ibrim, where countless documents written in
every language known in the Nile Valley have been found. The
elusive bilingual text has not emerged, however, and the rising
waters of Lake Nasser have percolated through the layers left there,
probably causing the destruction of much of the remaining organic
material.

Chapter 3
Hieroglyphs and art

Design of signs

Hieroglyphs had very specific purposes in Egypt. They were used for writing texts which were written for the gods, for an élite in the context of their relationship with the gods, and for the afterlife. Though hieroglyphs were used to write a recognizable language of Egypt, it was an exalted mode of communication within a formal ritual setting and within an architectural framework defining spatial and temporal zones. Most people were unable to read hieroglyphs and only a specialist group were ever taught the principles of the pictorial signs. The guiding principles for writing in hieroglyphs come from Egyptian art and ceremonial ideology rather than language. The purpose of the scribes in writing the hieroglyphic texts was quite specific, rarefied, and intellectually élitist.

Individual signs are generally recognizable as something from the Egyptian world. We might not recognize them straight away because we do not carry milk vessels on strings with us, nor are twisted flax fibres in everyday use, and nor do we come across vultures, guinea fowl, or horned vipers every day. Learning hieroglyphic signs is not only a linguistic exercise but, perhaps unexpectedly, it brings with it all kinds of cultural baggage to enable us to understand Egyptian culture and daily life.

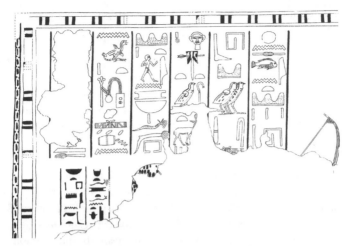

5. Hieroglyphs from the Tomb of Amenemhet, Thebes. Dating to Dynasty 18, each hieroglyph was a work of art, with the individual feathers of the birds being painted.

Signs are made recognizable by design. The artists who created the signs thought about the most recognizable form of the object which was being drawn. The human face can be seen both frontally, with its eyes and mouth, most apparent, or it can be seen in profile with the eye, nose, mouth, and chin being most prominent. The latter view was used as the hieroglyph for the Egyptian face. The principle of being able to recognize an object from its most obvious traits was used for every Egyptian image drawn in two dimensions. Birds are shown from the side, except for the owl, which has its flat face towards the viewer so that the distinctive shape of its head and eyes are clear. Roads are shown as a double line with protrusions on either side. These are meant to represent bushes growing along the roadside. The hieroglyph represents the road from above as a bird's eye view, with the bushes shown as stylized inverted triangles. This, too, is the rule for art – an object is drawn from a perspective that makes it most recognizable. A pool with trees around it is shown as seen from above with the trees flattened

39

against the ground. It may seem a strange perspective but is very logical.

Signs in context

The pictorial nature of writing allows it to blend with pictorial scenes on temple and tomb walls and the same principles governing the use of determinatives can also be applied at this larger scale, for example, in a temple wall register.

This scene from the Temple of Esna shows the king making an offering of two different types of sistra (musical rattles) to the goddesses Neith and Hathor. The figures are surrounded by lines of texts reading and proceeding in all directions. The texts concerned with the king read towards his face and are meant to emanate from him. The short vertical line directly in front of the king gives the title of the scene: 'Playing the sistra for the Two Ladies'. Above his head two cartouches identify the king; in this case he is actually the Roman emperor Titus. Behind him one vertical line of text reading left to right gives more of his virtues and attributes (the other vertical line reads the other way and belongs to the next scene to the

6. Offering scene from the Temple of Esna.

right). All the other texts in this scene read from right to left and give the speeches, the names and titles, and the rewards of the goddesses. Again one vertical column of text at the left frames this scene. The bands of text divide, label, give the words, and most importantly stress that the correct procedures for this offering and the correct mythical context have been evoked. Though the detail may differ from temple to temple and from scene to scene, each ritual is one compact action. It functions individually but it also works collectively within the temple wall, within this particular element of the building, within the whole complex, and within the whole cosmic environment. Each hieroglyph has its part to play architecturally and creatively. The writing provides the context for the scenes and the detail, but the huge scene acts as a determinative in a giant piece of writing so that the texts can be read correctly. The scene also shows the correct gestures and offering stance to be used in the performance of each ritual.

This is also the case with three-dimensional statuary. A statue of a man and his wife shows them seated but they are identified by texts, either at the base of the statue or written just behind them. The famous statue of Rahotep and Nofret, for example, has the husband and wife identified by their names written behind them on a back slab. In the case of Nofret, 'The Beautiful Woman', her image is identified by her name, with a female seated woman determining sign. The three-dimensional sculpture, however, itself acts as a huge determinative for the tiny piece of text. In the case of Rahotep, the relationship between sculpture and image is even more explicit. His titles and name are also written behind his head but his name does not have the accompanying seated male determinative. In this case, the compact text leads on to the statue itself acting as a Rahotep determinative, personified in stone as an ideal image of a man with his status. His spirit could easily have recognized its home, the image of its earthly body, reading the text, reading the statue, and taking up its residence from where it receives sustenance and revitalizes Rahotep in his next life.

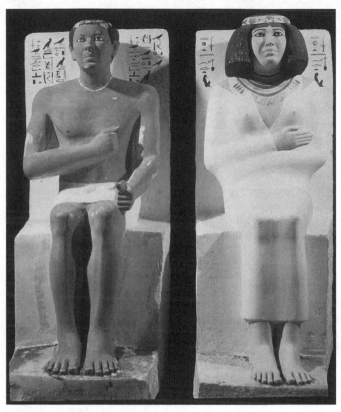

7. **Statue of Rahotep and Nofret, from Medum, Dynasty 4.**

Text and image are complementary and although the natural way for Egyptian to be written is from right to left, the pictorial qualities of hieroglyphs mean that the writing has much more flexible, architectural uses. One of the key elements in Egyptian design is the desire for symmetry, and the only way that this can be achieved with texts is by using hieroglyphs. The west wall of the tomb chapel of Werirenptah is now in the British Museum and comes originally from Saqqara, dating to Dynasty 5. It is dominated by two 'false' doors which were intended to be the access points to the living

42

world for the *kas* of Werirenptah and his wife, Khentkaues. Doorways are the entrances into important monuments such as tombs and temples, which are really entrances to different worlds, and so it was important for them to provide the right environment and a clear, pure entrance. The door jambs of the entrance are symmetrical, with the hieroglyphs facing one another on either side of the door. They help to focus attention on the actual door itself and complement the standing figures facing inward. In other entrances, especially in temples, the texts over the doorways were written symmetrically so that they would start in the centre of the door lintel. They read away from one another to the end of the lintel and then continue down the door jambs, still facing each other. This arrangement is aesthetically pleasing and provides a harmonized funnel focused towards the inside of the building or the room.

This architectural view and use of hieroglyphs is echoed in the zones and layout of funerary stelae. The limestone stela of the Guardian of the Chamber of Kheperka, Seru son of Sat-Hathor, is one of many hundreds of thousands made in Ancient Egypt, yet it speaks for all of them. It is rectangular and has a cavetto corniche – an architectural framing element found at the tops of doors and walls. The stela is divided in two by a vertical line of hieroglyphs containing the offering formula and reading in the normal direction from right to left. Both sides of the text are two symmetrical scenes. There are two horizontal lines of text on the right reading from left to right; on the left from right to left; then come two figures in silhouette facing each other inward, a man on the left (Seru) and a woman on the right (his mother, Sat-Hathor); then there are another six lines of text reading towards the edge of the stela. The two sides form the door leaves of a door designed to swing inwards. The figures would then both be inside the tomb, inside the realm of the dead, and would occupy their proper position. The hieroglyphic text would direct the offerer or visitor towards them, but turns out to be something different from the funerary formula down the centre, for it is a list of family members. This is a family monument

8. Stela of Seru in the Oriental Museum, University of Durham. Dated to Dynasty 12.

with as many people as possible mentioned on this one piece of stone so that they can have existence in the afterlife.

In looking at a wall covered in scenes and texts the most striking impression is that everything is well ordered in lines called registers. The scenes and texts are all written in straight lines. This may derive from the riverine nature of life in Egypt. The most common place to travel in Egypt would have been alongside or on the River Nile. From this perspective the whole world is ordered in horizontal registers: the river itself at the bottom, then a line of river bank, then a cultivated strip, then the trees, then the desert, and above the terrestrial sphere the sky. If this is viewed in the Egyptian way as a flat surface, then all of these elements are not arranged by perspective, one in front of the other, but in horizontal registers, one above the other. Within this context the lines of text fit well into scenes, interacting with the images depicted there or framing whole scenes. Most figures in a scene are accompanied by a line of hieroglyphs, usually identifying the person shown and often containing the words the figure is saying. The 'speech-balloon' always reads towards the face of the person speaking the words. In a temple, the king 'speaks' the offering ritual to the god of the temple and the gods reply with the appropriate reward speech. Even if the orientation of the texts at this point in the temple is left to right (for example, entering a room), the speech can be turned against this direction (retrograde) in order to suit a figure of the king coming through the door and speaking.[1] In more informal scenes the hieroglyphs record the more everyday speeches of ordinary people going about their daily business and reflect the positions of people as they face each other. Busy agricultural scenes in the tomb of Niankhkhnum and Khnumhotep record the words of agricultural workers, with the hieroglyphs acting like speech balloons in a cartoon strip. They provide a script to ensure that everyone in the scenes performs their role correctly, so that the tomb owner is not deprived of anything in his next life. The scenes may be to provide all the agricultural produce from seed to processed foodstuff in case the real offerings fail in the years ahead. Anybody who is anybody is

9. Catching fish in a trap, Tomb of Kagemni, Dynasty 5, Saqqara Necropolis.

named so that they can carry out their function. The scenes and text provide a memory of this life too, however idealized, so that the status of the tomb owners is also maintained and assured.

In the Tomb of Kagemni a boatman puts his fish trap into the water, hoping to land one of the many fish in the shallow waters. His words, *snḥw n pr-ḏt* 'Fish-trapping for the House of Eternity', leave no doubt as to the eventual destination of the fish. If all the hieroglyphs could be imagined as sound, the tombs would be full of noise, with the chatter of hundreds of people.

Perhaps in an even clearer illustration of words as pictures, the prayer for 'Drinking Water' in the afterlife is shown in the Tomb of Pashedu as hieroglyphic wall decoration, with the hieroglyphs of the prayer filling the air as his words float up into the air around him.

10. Pashedu in his tomb at Deir el Medina, Thebes, from Dynasty 19. The words of his prayer float up into the air around him like a designer wallpaper.

Proportion and aesthetic variation

For practical purposes the lines of hieroglyphic texts had to be able
to fit into the spaces allocated for them. The versatility of the
hieroglyphic script and the artistic sense of proportion of those who
drew the hieroglyphs mean that there is hardly ever a space at the
end of a line of a monumental text where the hieroglyphs ran out
and could not fill up the register, and nor do the hieroglyphs
become smaller towards the end of the line as the artist tried to
cram them all into an ever diminishing space. Of course there are
examples of texts from elite monuments where this does occur, but
in so many areas of wall and stone surface it shows that even
Egyptian artisans sometimes miscalculated, had breaks, or
changed their minds. Lines of text were written from the beginning
with aesthetic principles as one of the most important driving
factors. Firstly, imagine the area covered by a large hieroglyph
as being divided into four small squares. Then almost every
sign will fit into those spaces and be either small and squat
(one square), long and horizontal or vertical (two squares), or
large (four squares).

Individual words tend to be able to fit into a rectangle or square
area. For example, the writing of the word 'strong' is made up from
the following signs: ∿∿∿⊘◠𓢐 all vertically compact signs,
with the longer horizontal first and last signs. This could be written:
⊘◠𓢐 combining groups in small square units to take up less
space and look more aesthetically pleasing. Nevertheless, it retains
the order in which the signs are read. If the space available was very
small, however, it could be written: 𓏏𓂝. In order to accommodate
such variability signs sometimes had to be written in different sizes,
but as long as they were still recognizable, it was fine. Sometimes
the actual writing of words could be shortened or changed in order
to make the word fit into the space available. There were also space-
filling vertical strokes to fill up the awkward gaps. 𓄤𓍖 'beautiful' is
often abbreviated to 𓄤 alone, especially in epithets, where a short,
pithy writing is desirable.

ꜣꜥꜣ⌣ *b3* 'to hack up earth' can be written more imaginatively and using less space as 𓎉, but with exactly the same meaning.

As in most languages until the recent past there was no uniform way to spell words in Egyptian, so that some variation was possible. It is clear that for certain words there were definite ways in which they could be written and ways in which they were never written, so that students did have to learn some spellings. For example, 'to hear' is usually written ⌒𓄿 or ⌒𓄿𓏛, but hardly ever 𓂋𓏏𓄿⌒𓏛 which would be the way of spelling it with monoconsonantal signs.

In fact, it was not only words which were subject to variation; even individual signs could appear visually different. The pictorial quality of the signs underlies another important principle of Egyptian hieroglyphs, that of the possibility of variation in signs which might or might not have an influence on the meaning of the sign and its use. In a recent study of First Intermediate Period stelae from Gebelein and Naga ed-Deir, Sabine Kubisch collected together all the examples of the hieroglyph used to write the word *wdpw*, 'cup-bearer', and the variation is remarkable. The fifteen examples of this hieroglyph all show the same basic thing, a man standing and holding out a cup, but they are all different. The man is more or less bent over, his arm holding the cup is straight or bent, he may hold a second vessel in his other hand, he may pour liquid from a vessel into the cup, or he holds the two vessels high up into the air. Here, away from the eagle eye of the conformists at court, the local artists drew whatever they wanted, but each of these variations seems to mean exactly the same thing. The differences are not significant for the reading of the word. They may be due to a deliberate choice on the part of the scribes to make each sign different, to the fact that different people had different ways of rendering this particular sign, or to the fact that even individuals are inconsistent about what they do. The 'Dancing Men' deciphered by Sherlock Holmes formed a cryptic script where each pose had a precise and different meaning. There is no better example than this to show the way in which Egyptian differs from cryptic scripts and

49

how hieroglyphs can have a vagueness in their detail.[2] The reader had to be aware of when such differences might have meaning and when they might not. For example, ⌐ an arm and hand holding a stick is very different in potential meaning (determinative for 'strength' or violent action) from an arm and hand holding a specific staff or sceptre, ⌐ (supervising actions). On the other hand the sign 𓀢 is also a determinative for 'strength' or violent actions. The standing man is a tall vertical sign and the arm long and horizontal, so that the space available in the whole writing of the word may have affected the choice of sign. But was there really any difference in their meaning? Knowledge of such differences came through practice and experience and had to be learnt.

Literacy and access

Most of the Egyptian population were field workers, herdsmen, or craftsmen who lived in dispersed agricultural settlements up and down the Nile Valley and in the less marshy delta areas. They lived off what they grew, supplied surpluses for the royal and temple landowners and had access to good supplies of basic commodities at a local level. They did not have access to the resources of the élite, including the ability to have stone tomb monuments for their personal commemoration. As many hieroglyphic texts were written in monumental contexts such as tombs and temples the mass of Egyptians had restricted access to them. It has been estimated from the occurrence of élite monuments with writing on them that in the Old Kingdom only around 1 per cent of the population was literate, that is, could read and write at all, and possibly for hieroglyphs the figure was even lower. At the most basic level, the ability to read and write one's name may have been more widespread, particularly for administrative purposes, and this writing would almost certainly have been in hieratic not hieroglyphs.

The tombs of the élite were often in special necropolis areas. In the Nile Valley this would frequently be the desert edge, perhaps visited only by close relatives who took part in funerary offerings and feasts and in the performance of rituals. If they were of the same social standing they might read and may even have recognized themselves and other people depicted in the tomb. The son of the dead man (or a literate substitute) would have had to be able to recite an offering prayer for his father. On the outer door jambs and lintels of some tombs or in funerary stelae there are sometimes specific calls to the passer-by to make sure that the offerings are continued in the tomb for the dead person's *ka*. They begin, 'O all the living who pass by or who enter in this tomb . . .', and may have been intended to function after the immediate family had passed away and were no longer able to continue the cult. Once the living had departed, the writing and its properties were intended to function, continually activating and providing the food and necessary goods for the dead person in the afterlife. Ultimately, the audience was only the spirits (*kas*) of the dead and they depended on the few *ka*-priests and lector priests whose job it was to read out the relevant rituals. For the visitors to such places, the visual impact must have been very striking, a marker of a sacred zone with messages about status and life after death.

In temples the audience was even more restricted. 'Ordinary' Egyptians were not allowed into the temple complexes as they were impure. The priests appointed as 'servants of the gods' were specifically supposed to be purified before they entered the temple. Once inside, they performed rituals to ensure that the temple god was cared for and enjoyed regular meals and festivals. Many of the special prayers and rites were written on the walls and in papyrus scrolls from which they were read out by the 'lector-priest'. Some of the prayers could have been learned by heart, so that even a priest who served only a short time in the temple may have needed relatively little ability to read the texts on the walls. In any case, much of the temple would have been dark and gloomy, with only the play of light through the narrow openings in the roof onto small sections of the wall at any one time, or the flicker of lamplight on the walls, to illuminate the texts. They were, after all, intended for the eyes of the gods and for them alone. In this case, hieroglyphs

51

truly are 'the words of the gods', providing the medium of communication between the ordinary world and the supernormal.

The presence of hieroglyphs acts as a status marker. The most extreme form of status, being divine, implied an all-embracing knowledge and magical power which could interact with the scenes and texts on temple walls. The rituals activated the hieroglyphs, so that by the scent and smoke of burning incense the very writing could be inhaled by the gods; poured water soaked into the offerings and the fabric of the temple, energizing and bringing life; the provision of food, with its smells and taste, activated the senses and power of the gods. Not just each single hieroglyph, but also the two-dimensional reliefs, the three-dimensional statues, and the physical enactments and rituals were all 'read' to fulfil the function of the temple. In a way, each was also a back-up for the other, should they fail for some reason. The pragmatic Egyptians realized that in order to make the house of the god endure after they had gone, they needed the medium of writing to continue their work. In essence, the temple walls continue to provide the energy for the gods and the hieroglyphs continue, even to this day, before the innocent eyes of tourists and guardians, to mediate with the gods of Egypt.

The exterior walls of the temples presented a different world and the acres of space on the high, stone enclosures of temples with the impressive mountain-like pylons as the entrance gave a huge canvas for scenes and texts. They were decorated with very particular scenes which served a purpose in terms of the cosmic dimension of the temple and perhaps as a giant advertising hoarding for those on the outside. These scenes showed the king destroying his enemies and the forces of chaos before the gods, either by personally dispatching them or by fighting them in battles. In vivid colours, made luminescent in the strong Egyptian sunlight, they would have provided a gaudy and living panoply of war and conquest to anyone within the temple complex. More people were allowed into this part of the temple than into the inner house of the god. The message of these advertisements is that the king had conquered his foes, chaos had been removed to the outside of the temple realm, and *maat*, 'cosmic harmony', was maintained.

Technically, the small print was irrelevant. The viewer could take in the message in one glance, but it was still inscribed for the gods themselves to read. These texts hardly need any hieroglyphs, yet they have them, identifying individuals, describing the scenes, listing the names of the defeated enemy and giving the tallies of the dead and captured in the battle scenes. Such images occupy their proper place and give the message that the king is fulfilling his part of the bargain with the gods by keeping chaos at bay. As a result, everyone could be reassured that the gods would continue to allow the Nile inundation to come and the sun to continue its daily cycle across the heavens. In the Egyptian psyche, this may have meant that the investment of the Egyptian people in the power of their king was worth it, as it was proved to work. The giant hieroglyphs spell out the bargain of man and gods and the control of the king over his Egyptian people.

Inevitably, the status conferred by writing is most powerfully felt nearest to the king and the court. The tombs of his officials are covered in writing. As one moves away from this power base it is possible to see what has been termed a more 'provincial' type of writing and hieroglyphs. It has been suggested that examples of 'provincial' art and writing occurred mostly at times when central authority in the country was weakening and local provincial governors took on a role and status more like those at the central royal court. The style of art shows a lack of proportion in the drawing of figures: they have disproportionately large heads with huge eyes, the body is drawn in a stick-like fashion, and the quality of the hieroglyphs is bad. The text can be written randomly and without baselines or structured register lines and they can be so poorly drawn that they are sometimes scarcely recognizable. The funerary stelae of the governors of Dendera and the nomes of Middle Egypt during the First and Second Intermediate periods show these tendencies. Nevertheless the functions of these pieces of

11. Stela of Montuhotep, from Er-Rizeqat, Middle Egypt, Second Intermediate Period.

writing remains the same. While they may not preserve the aesthetic merit of the Saqqara necropolis two or three hundred miles away, for people who would never have the chance to leave their home village or town this writing was as real as it could be. After all, in modern times tourists are happy to come away from their holiday destinations with locally produced papyri or to wear fashionable clothes adorned with kanji characters which they cannot read or understand. The love of the exotic, the personally meaningful, and the aesthetically pleasing is a human quality which persists through the ages.

At Er-Rizeqat a man called Montuhotep employed an artist to produce a fitting monument for him. The artist produced a vibrantly coloured stela that would give him status and enhance his local standing – and anyone who had never seen such a stela would be no wiser as to its quality. The fact of its existence, with linear hieroglyphs and not full hieroglyphic script, was enough for personal propaganda purposes, both in this life and the next.

Chapter 4

'I know you, I know your names'
Coffin Texts, Spell 407

A number of papyrus fragments and other texts from the New Kingdom preserve the story of 'The Cunning of Isis'. As the consort and sister of Osiris, Isis had great magical abilities, including that of being able to revivify the mummified body of her husband sufficiently to enable her to conceive their son, Horus. As the avenger of his father, Horus was embodied in the person of the king of Egypt. The role of Isis in this important ideological framework was paramount and 'The Cunning of Isis' gives a mythological version of how she came to gain her magical powers. Isis manufactured a serpent from mud mixed with the spittle of the sun god, Re, who at the time of this tale (perhaps in the evening) was old and tending to drool. She left the serpent on the pathway where the sun god would walk each day. When Re passed by, the serpent stirred and stung the god. Serpent bites are not necessarily fatal and especially not to sun gods, but they can hurt and Re was in agony. Isis, as the healer, came to see her father and diagnosed a serpent bite. She claimed, however, that she could only cure Re if he told her his secret name: 'A man lives when one recites in his name.'[1] Re, in fact, had many names and forms. He had one name for each hour of the day and perhaps more than that, but he also had a secret name which gave him invincibility. In order to remove the pain, Re whispered his names to Isis and she accordingly constructed a spell, including the names to take away the pain. She knew, however, that Re would never give up his hidden name so easily and therefore her spell was ineffective. She went back to her father and said that as he had not told her his true 'secret' name, the pain would continue. This time Re gave in and whispered his true secret name to her, which she incorporated into her spell. It then worked, releasing the sun god from his agony. At the end of this episode, Re was healed, but Isis still knew the secret name of Re. The implication of the myth is that this was the basis of her power.

This colourful story, full of allusion and subtlety, like most Egyptian myths, is founded on the basic principle that the name of a person contains the essence of that person. In addition, the knowledge of the name can invoke the being of an individual for good or for bad. For those people who were of sufficient status to have their names written in hieroglyphs, the extra magical power of the hieroglyphs was a potent mixture. A statue or relief sculpture or drawing could be an image of anyone. As soon as it was identified with a name, written in hieroglyphs or hieratic, it gave identity to that image and image to that individual. Like the grammatical determinative, it determined 'who' a person was. In part, this explains the idealized images which we associate with Egyptian art. The lithe men and women portrayed in statues and the portly officials at work in their tombs are not 'portraits' of real people but ideal images of themselves as persons of rank and status identified by their names and titles. Portraits do exist but within the framework created by this principle. The name means that the image can be recognized by various entities and this is of paramount importance in the tomb and funerary context and also in the temple, both the main arenas for the writing of hieroglyphs.

In the tomb chapel, the cult of the deceased was maintained by priests and relatives after the death of the tomb owner. Here they made food and liquid offerings and burnt incense, nourishing the spirit of the dead in the afterlife and stimulating their senses. However, the focal parts of the cult, the false door, stela, and offering table, all contain the name of the dead and these elements provide the point of contact with the dead and with the 'correct' individual, labelled by the hieroglyphs. From the other side of the afterlife, the *ka* and the *ba* recognized this refuelling point by the hieroglyphs naming the particular person. The hieroglyphs communicate the correct information and ensure that the dead continue to be fed, watered and anointed in the afterlife.

Within the temple, the images of the gods were named on the walls, ensuring that they took part in the correct rituals and took their places in the cosmic symmetry of the temple. To some extent, the naming of these images brings them to life, activates them and makes the roving essence of the gods immanent within their images, be they falcon statues, as at Edfu Temple, or Hathor reliefs, as at Dendera. It seems to have been important that each being was in its correct place.

The opposite of this idea was also appreciated by the Egyptians. If it were true that hieroglyphs in themselves were images of animals, people, birds, and even reptiles and that hieroglyphs were imbued with some kind of animating power, could it not also be the case that these creatures could come to life on the tomb walls where they were written? In this case might they not threaten the dead person and their continued existence? Indeed, this was believed to be the case and in the Pyramid Texts of Dynasty 5 written inside the burial chambers of the pyramids of kings such as Teti or Pepi I, the animal hieroglyphs were individually mutilated. The animal signs were written without legs, birds had their heads cut off, knives were inserted into the bodies of snakes or crocodiles, human figures were drawn incomplete, and sometimes certain signs were completely substituted if they could not be disabled in some other way.

Taking this idea further, the complete removal of the name of a person could also remove their existence. If the name of a tomb owner were scratched away, his *ka* would not recognize its images and could not be nourished and therefore the dead person would not live in the afterlife. Their name, the memory of them, and their cult would indeed be forgotten and their being would be inanimate. Clearly, this was an act of condemnation, sending a person to their second death, the most feared end for any human life. It was used in Egypt against both human beings and gods as a political and religious act of denial of existence.

Hatshepsut ruled Egypt on behalf of her stepson, Thutmose III, and assumed the full regalia and titles of 'King'. Yet, some time after her death her names and images were scratched out from many of the temples she had built and even in her mortuary temple, designed to continue her afterlife existence. The exact reasons for this can only be guessed at, but the effect is undeniable. Someone was trying to erase her memory, so that she would not exist in the minds or eyes of people in this life or in the next. Similarly, after the reign of Akhenaten, his name and images were systematically removed from his city at Akhetaten and also from his monuments at Karnak.

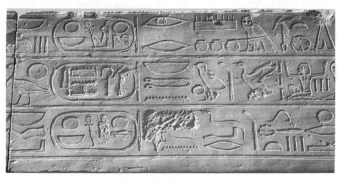

12. Examples of the erasure of the name of Amun from the architraves of a colonnade in Luxor Temple.

The *damnatio memoriae* had been a favourite weapon of Akhenaten himself during his reign when he turned to the worship of the sun disk, the Aten, and apparently away from the previous state god, Amun. He had ordered the removal of the name of Amun from wherever it occurred, particularly in the heartland of the god at Thebes and among the supporters of the old religio-political order. Many of them had names compounded with the name of Amun, such as 'Amun-em-het', 'Amun is to the front', and even his father had been called 'Amun-hotep', 'Amun is content'. Nothing was safe and Amun was scratched out in tombs and temples, on statues and objects in a truly literal gesture of 'rubbing him out'. In the context of the tombs it almost casually removed the afterlife existence of the person too.

The denial of existence was a strong political gesture in a culture where such beliefs permeated political and social situations and institutions. It seems to have been one of the worst things which could be done to a person and the fact that so many texts mention the hope that names will continue to exist suggests that the fear of losing the written name went deep. Even Akhenaten himself acknowledged it in his boundary stela at Akhetaten, saying of the inscription, 'It shall not be scratched out, it shall not be washed off, it shall not be hacked out, it shall not be washed over with gypsum-plaster. It shall not be lost and if it is lost, if it disappears, or if the stela on which it is falls down, I shall renew it again as a new thing in this place where it is'.[2]

Power and the written word

In magical rituals the gestures, dancing, incantation, smoke, and magical objects were not enough to make some spells work. They needed the extra power of written hieroglyphs. A lector priest's toolkit from a Middle Kingdom tomb under the Ramesseum at Thebes consisted of a box containing all the paraphernalia for invoking power. There were fertility figures, ivory 'wands' covered in bizarre and fantastic creatures, a cowherd figure, a copper serpent, and a figure of a woman wearing a lioness mask and holding two serpent wands in her hands. Together with these objects were papyri covered in texts in hieratic, including literary works and magical texts. Whoever owned this box was a trained scribe with a sideline or maybe a job in providing magical services for people at Thebes. It is the association of the gear and the written material which is so fascinating. This person, most likely to be a man, possibly with a female helper as suggested by the lioness-masked figure, would have been called out to help in times of births, to offer fertility rituals, to offer cures in the case of snake or scorpion bites or other afflictions. The written spells could provide the authority for the rest of the activities and no doubt there were specific incantations for specific purposes.[3]

In a more sinister light there is a class of object from Egypt called 'Execration Figures'. They were made of mud or stone and were often in the form of enemy prisoners with their hands tied behind their backs. They would have spells against 'enemies', or 'ills', written on their bodies and then they would be broken and smashed into pieces, so that the named enemies were completely destroyed. It is possible that these figures relate to general ills and evils, especially as a kind of perceived threat from 'foreigners', and so they are a general protection for Egyptians. They are a more institutionalized form of racist hatred or fear, particularly as shown in the horrifying Mirgissa burial of a decapitated Nubian with all the hallmarks of a ritual slaughter, accompanied by magic. The ritual most likely involved a set of prescribed gestures and spoken words read out from a scroll or recited from memory. It is no accident that from the Ptolemaic and Roman periods it is the god of writing, Thoth, who is most closely associated with magical ritual, surviving into medieval thought as Hermes Trismegistus.

The inherent power of hieroglyphs to transform themselves or animate is adopted in the Memphite story of the creation of the world. Here, Ptah was believed to have first created everything by simply thinking of the names of things, then speaking their names.

At the moment of his speaking the names of things and beings they came into existence and the world was created with all its plants, people, and animals. It is perhaps significant that this 'Memphite Theology' survives, copied onto stone supposedly from an older 'worm-eaten' papyrus scroll now lost. The stone was inscribed in the reign of the Nubian king, Shabako (712–702 BC) and highlights the interest of the later rulers in the 'ancient' writings of the past.[4] The Demotic story cycle of Setne Khaemwese centres on the search for a book written by Thoth himself which contained two powerful spells. According to the story, the reader of this book would be able to charm all the cosmos and understand the words of birds and reptiles, perhaps a metaphorical allusion to being able to understand hieroglyphs.[5]

Playing with words, text, and signs

For the priests with the ability to read hieroglyphs and trained to copy and edit ancient texts in the 'House of Life' it was just not enough to ensure that the meaning was preserved and that the exact rituals were continued. They introduced extra hieroglyphs into the writing system, swelling the number of signs used from a core of about 750 in Middle Egyptian to over 7,000 in the texts of the Ptolemaic Temples. A text in basic Middle Egyptian grammar would then appear to be unreadable to someone trained only in Middle Egyptian hieroglyphs:

From the exterior of the naos of the Temple of Edfu, Ptolemaic Period (Chassinat, *Edfou*, VI, 2,4–5).

Transcription of above text into Middle Egyptian hieroglyphs.

Translation: 'He rises from Nun, he sails the heavens as Hor-Akhty, he stands in the sky opposite it (the temple) every day'.

Is it really more cryptic? It is certainly more abbreviated, but there are interesting mythical allusions in the writings: the word for the primeval ocean, 'Nun', is written in Ptolemaic signs, with a child over the water sign, perhaps hinting at the primeval lotus child emerging from the first waters. The word *nww* later *nn* is a New Kingdom word for 'child', so the determinative acquires the value *nwn* and is given the water-canal determinative to complete the writing; the words for 'every day' at the end are written with the sun god Re and the moon god Khonsu – sun and moon, a striking image of exactly what is meant.

In other texts, the temple rituals are expanded and do not occur in such a fully written form earlier. Variations and extra signs were added with some imagination and the ways in which the 'new' signs were developed took into consideration a number of different 'rules'.

First, more and more determinatives were turned into simple monoconsonantal phonetic signs. For example, the sign ꓮ, a man with his arms held up in the air, can be the determinative written at the end of the word for *hꜥꜥ* 'haa', to rejoice; so in Ptolemaic, ꓮ acquires the sound value of *h* and is written within other words just with this sound value: ꓮ ꟽ in the name of the god Heka in the Temple of Esna (Esna 242,18). Of course, ꓮ is also the determinative of *kꜣ* 'ka', to be high, and so can take on the value *k* and indeed another writing of the word of the god Heka, also at Esna, is the picturesque ꓮ ꓮ ꟽ (Esna 242, 24).

Secondly, signs capable of carrying or wearing something, did so and in the process acquired another value: ꟽ a seated man holding a horned viper above his head is read as *fꜣi*, meaning 'to raise up' and the viper has the value *f*. This group really reads *fꜣi = f* and the emphasis of *f* gives the value of the whole group *f*.

Some fewer signs were complete puns in their own right: � and ꞷ form a pair showing the viper 'leaving' the sign and then 'going

63

into' the sign. They are the writings for *pr* 'to go out' and ⸌*k*
'enter'.

The sign of the man holding the hippopotamus by the tail 𓀀 is
used in the writing of the word for lapis lazuli and so has the
reading *ḥsdb*, though this in itself is a later version of the word *ḥsbd*
from Dynasty 18. The writing is a punning sign-play, studied in
1876 by W. Goodwin. He suggested that here the man is performing
the action *ḥs*(*f*) 'driving away', and the object of his attention is *db*
'the hippopotamus', so the phrase *ḥs*(*f*) *db* 'driving away the
hippopotamus' sounded the same as or similar to the word for lapis
lazuli and the signs making up this tableau were used in the writing
for the substance. It is also possible that the protective powers of
lapis are symbolically invoked here, so that amulets of lapis could be
used to drive away danger and evil, here represented by the
hippopotamus.

The possibilities for such games with signs and sound values mean
that sportive texts occur quite often, particularly in 'religious' or
'funerary' texts as early as the Old Kingdom, and they are not
confined to the Ptolemaic and Roman periods. It has been said
that the priests of these times wished to make the Egyptian texts
for which they were responsible more difficult for others to read
and to try to hide the 'truths' which they contained. As the texts
could only ever have been read by a small group of people and as
the ruling Greek administrators would have been excluded from
reading any hieroglyphs anyway this seems to be a specious
argument. In fact, the mythological texts, the temple unguent and
perfume recipes, the list of library books, and in particular the
ritual texts are not written in especially 'cryptic' hieroglyphs at all.
The cryptic texts are those very much in prominent places, such as
on window frames or architraves – high up, addressing the gods,
and almost on show for all to marvel at the intricacies of the script
and the erudition of the language. They consist of descriptions,
basic acts of ritual, and nothing particularly secret. The cryptic
texts rely upon double meanings of signs or signs which represent

13. Crocodile hymn to Sobek, written in crocodile signs, Temple of Esna.

what they stand for and they are the best example of the ideographic script believed in by occultists and the early decipherers of hieroglyphs.

Perhaps the most extreme examples of cryptography are two texts in the temple of Esna. They are hymns to the crocodile god, Sobek-Re, and the ram god, Khnum, and they can be seen in the Roman pronaos (the front part of the temple), on the inside of a doorway. When the light hits them, the texts are revealed in all their mischievous glory, for the Sobek hymn is written almost entirely in crocodiles and the Khnum hymn in ram hieroglyphs.

Luckily, the Sobek hymn begins with the words 'Praise to Sobek' and then continues in crocodiles. It is clearly a hymn of praise and seems to consist of epithets of the god, extolling his various qualities and attributes, even his crocodileness. From other texts, the crocodile sign has a wide range of possible uses and readings, such as 'lord', 'power of attack', 'divine', 'Sobek', 'appearing in glory', 'time', 'one who seizes', and so on.[6] The clever thing about the hymns is that the priests who wrote them used the whole hymn as a symbolic message, for both gods are recognized as creator gods, who created everything themselves and are immanent in everything. Therefore, the hymns express the idea that divinity exists in everything through the medium of meaning, sound value, writing, and representation. If one text were needed to express the real triumph of hieroglyphs it would be one of these two.

If such texts hint at the same kind of fun as that to be had in compiling a crossword, there are genuine 'acrostic' texts which can be read in at least two directions. A stela in the tomb of Nebwenenef, from the beginning of the reign of Ramesses II, bears a standard hymn to Osiris and Re written in horizontal lines. Halfway along a pair of vertical lines are drawn down the stela, enclosing one group of hieroglyphs from each line between them. This constitutes a short vertical text. A hymn to Mut on the stela of Paser from the reign of Ramesses VI has taken the process further by writing out every word of a hymn in a squared grid. Two hymns can be read horizontally and vertically. The text actually refers to a third reading which may have been around the outside, though this part of the stela is now lost and so cannot be read.[7]

There are texts which appear to be written in sportive hieroglyphs but may not be. A stela now in the Louvre (Stela C12) contains a usual funerary inscription for the first few lines of the text and then there is an extraordinary row of figures, carved at about double the height of the usual lines of text. These figures seem to be grouped in a small tableau but they are doing or carrying bizarre things. One man carries a human head on a tray, another wears a mask, and a group of headless beings run along together. This is not usual behaviour for images on such stela or for texts. Could it be a depiction of some strange rituals carried out at Osiris festivals? Could it be a misunderstood copy of some much older text? Étienne Drioton, who was a master of Ptolemaic writing, saw in this line of figures a line of cryptic texts and proposed a translation for it based on his principles of how such writings were achieved in Egypt.[8]

There are also examples of whole statues containing word plays or a rebus. In a statue in Cairo Museum, Ramesses II is shown as a child wearing a solar disk on his head, clutching a reed plant in his hand, and squatting in front of a Horus falcon. Some of the imagery is standard, such as the Horus falcon protecting the king, but the king as a child is more unusual and the reed plant at first seems out of place. As the statue is a rebus it should be read as a phrase where the hieroglyphic elements are: the sun disk, the child, and the reed. They are the signs reading R^c-ms-sw, 'Ramesses', 'The sun god Re bore him', the name of the king. This was not a new idea and some of the statues of Senenmut, the high official of Hatshepsut, play similar word games: a man offers a cobra with a pair of arms on its head and a solar disk. This is the word 'Maat-ka-re', one of the names of 'King' Hatshepsut herself, so her highest official dedicates her to the gods.

In some small way, hieroglyphic texts are constantly invoking extra meaning and symbolism and in ways which we can only barely appreciate. One of the most frequent forms of word plays in texts is the use of onomatopoeia and alliteration in rituals and other texts. At the minimum this is where a string of words beginning with the same sound are combined in an alliterative phrase: 'Peter Piper picked a peck of pickled pepper.' It can be further refined where words containing the same sounds are combined: 'Ten taut taws taught Taurus the tawdry truth.' The final version of this system is the development of the pun, where two words sound the same but have widely different meanings, often used in English for humour: 'Infamy! Infamy! They've all got it in for me!'[9] All of these *double entendres*, puns, and sound games are used in Ptolemaic and Roman temple texts, though perhaps without the humorous element. In fact, most often punning is treated as an elevated form of expression and of divine communication: *wḏȝ r wḏȝt nb wḏȝw m ꜥ = i* 'wedja er wedjat neb wedjau em aai', 'Proceeding to every room, amulets in my hands', literally meaning 'Going safely to every safe place, safety-things in my hands'. There is no doubt that the underlying meaning is a sense of protection and preservation. The sounds repeated reinforce the meaning and emphasize the underlying message. This is particularly important in destroying enemy powers, so alliteration and puns are vital in rituals of this kind: *ḫftyw ḫbḫb m ḥmt* 'kheftiu khebkheb em khemet', 'the enemies are destroyed with the harpoon'. They can also be used to affirm good things: *mȝꜥ mȝꜥt* 'Offering maat'.

This last example is also the basis of one of the most important puns in Edfu Temple. This is a temple concerned with the cosmic order and the role of the Egyptian kingship within it, at the centre of it. The concept of '*maat*' as 'cosmic harmony', 'truth', and 'justice' is well known, but it is the central ritual in the temple demonstrating the link and the bargain between humans and gods which is balanced by the king in the middle as the intermediary. It is also the focus of a series of puns where the offering of *maat* is reinforced. The way in which '*maat*' was actually spoken seems to have sounded more like 'mere' and it is close in sound to Egyptian words for 'throat', 'songstress', 'what he loves', and 'eye'. The mention of all of these things independently can also bring to mind the central idea of *maat*, with each one incorporating all the aspects of the other ideas. There is a central theme, that of the throat providing song and access to the body for nourishment, which is one of the aims of *maat*. When the goddess Hathor is called *maat*, however, the name invokes her roles as songstress, as the nourisher of the king, as his beloved, and as his all-seeing eye. Puns of this kind have a vital purpose to preserve the power of the things they name. Hearing an Egyptian ritual must have been as much an aural and intellectual experience as it was physical, smelling the incense, seeing the gestures, hearing the voices. The play on words and ideas stimulated and engaged all the senses at once.

How lucky the gods were.

Chapter 5
Scribes and everyday writing

The creation of a hieroglyphic text, with each individual feather of the bird signs and each basket carefully carved in stone and then painted as well, needed the attentions of a team of craftsmen. Following the composition of the required text probably onto a papyrus roll, it would have first been written in red ink on a prepared wall surface (the work of stonemasons and line setters), then a master draughtsman would have overwritten the text in black ink, using the red text as his guide to the space required and the signs to be used in words. At this stage he would have a perfect idea of exactly where each sign fitted and how large it needed to be to fill the allocated space. In essence, the master was creating a text no less time-consuming, but this time it was perfect.

Then the sculptors moved in. If it were to be raised relief, standing proud of the surface of the stone, the background would have to be cut back, so first the less-skilled team moved in to block out the larger empty areas. As they moved closer to the signs, more-skilled sculptors took over, carving closer and closer around the outlines of the sign and finally moulding and incising details upon each hieroglyph. Finally, the painters, probably with their own allotted colours, would work their way along the wall or monument. As they went by, this ancient wave of colour processors would activate the scene in blue, yellow, red-brown, and white.

If the scene was to be carved in sunk relief, this faster process required only the actual signs to be cut back as in the rough, undetailed work of the Amarna temple and private stela reliefs. The cut-back signs, however, often accompanied sunk-relief art, with its surfaces modelled and moulded as if they were made of plaster. The position of the text could also dictate the type of relief required. Texts and images on the outside of buildings or monuments were usually written in sunk relief in order to catch the raking or direct sunlight. Texts inside buildings or enclosed areas were usually carved in raised relief so that they were highlighted by faint lamplight or any light which might come in through the doorway or roof openings.

The creators of such hieroglyphic texts required skill and practice. There were also different levels of craftsmen and some such as the painters and sculptors would not have been able to read the texts they were creating. This is reflected in the terms used for the people involved. The word for a scribe in Egyptian is *sš* (*sḫ*) and this is also applied to 'writings' with the papyrus roll determinative. The inscriber of hieroglyphs was called *gnwty* 'sculptor' and the actions of writing in ink and carving in stone were regarded as very different skills.

Scribes and hieratic

For the average scribe making tax returns in a delta village which had to be in by the end of the month, the hieroglyphic script was not a practical option. Instead, the administrative bureaucracy used the shorthand, cursive script known as hieratic. The scribe would sit cross-legged on the ground or a low stool, with his kilt pulled tight over his knees to create a table. His papyrus roll would be unrolled at the required place and a page left open. The left end would have been held by the scribe's left hand; the right may have been weighted down or allowed to fall to the right, keeping the papyrus taut. Taking his reed brush in his hand, the scribe would dip the brush in his water pot, then onto a cake of ink, mix until the black was perfect, and then paint his hieratic letters swiftly from right to left along the horizontal fibres exposed on the open side of the papyrus. The fibres formed a natural ruled line, keeping his lines of writing straight. The beginning of texts or important parts were written in red ink, the other colour on his palette. The method of holding the pen was more like holding a brush, with the reed pen lightly balanced on the second, third, and fourth fingers and guided by the thumb with the hand held above the surface of the papyrus. This meant that the cursive hieroglyphs could be written (or painted) even more quickly.

This idyllic picture presupposes that all scribes were right-handed and indeed they are usually shown as right-handed. It is not clear if it was a requirement for the profession or not, but it is more natural for right-handed people to start writing where their hand falls on the page, at the right-hand side, and move away to the left. Further, in the Old and Middle Kingdom, hieratic texts tended to be written in vertical columns, starting at the right and working to the left. It is not known if this was simply a fashion or whether it represented a scribal school connected with the location of the political centre of the country. In the Middle Kingdom it was based at Itj-Tawy in the Fayum area and by the New Kingdom it had moved to Thebes and Memphis. By late Dynasty 12 writing in horizontal lines had come in and was to become more usual in everyday papyrus documents after this time. The vertical column style is retained for some religious documents such as the *Books of the Dead* and may have been regarded as a deliberately archaic practice.

Looking at a hieratic text, it is sometimes easy to see the pictorial hieroglyphs from which the signs derive. Whereas the sign for the seated man would involve carving the hieroglyphs in several stages, the hieratic reduces the number of times the reed brush needs to come to the surface of the papyrus or writing board or ostrakon. A seated-man hieroglyph requires his head, body, arms, and legs to be drawn out carefully, while the hieratic version is a backwards S-shape with a vertical line drawn through it, completed in

Sign 1: From a Dynasty 6 letter. The owl retains its ears and is still more a linear sign.

Sign 2: From the Dynasty 18 Book of the Dead of Nakht. This is a true linear hieroglyph.

Sign 3: From the Dynasty 19 Papyrus Chester Beatty I, 'Struggle Between Horus and Seth'. The sign is now made in one movement and retains the sense of the head and body, but the distinctive ears and talons have gone.

Sign 4: From the beginning of the New Kingdom, Papyrus Edwin Smith. A smoother, more elegant version of the hieratic *m*.

14. Examples of the owl sign in various types or dates of hieratic writing, all reading from right to left.

two or three quick, flowing strokes. An owl hieroglyph could have incredibly detailed feathering in its hieroglyphic form, yet in hieratic it is reduced to one flowing movement and looks like a 3. Certain groups of signs were put together in ligatures, so that they could be written in one or two strokes rather than several separate movements.

While it is true that hieroglyphic styles can be differentiated, they are always going to be the product of teamwork and so the hand of an individual craftsman often cannot be identified except after careful study of hand-painted hieroglyphs. Documents written in hieratic must always be the work of an individual and they preserve all kinds of handwriting. Depending on the type of document, there are some beautiful examples of what might be called a 'book hand', such as the Ramesside Papyrus Harris I, which is complete with painted vignettes. There are also some examples of student texts, or simply texts written by a bad scribe, and there is a whole range of material in between. At least these are truly holograph versions of these documents, whoever may have written them. The study of the handwriting (palaeography) is useful in dating texts as there are noticeable differences in styles over time. This is true for any handwritten document, but in Egypt it is particularly useful for documents without a provenance or which have been reused later. The style of dated documents is studied and the characteristics of the handwriting can be applied to documents of unknown date. Through this type of study individuals can be recognized and this in turn can have implications for following individual careers and sometimes state affairs.

An archive of letters written by the scribe of the tomb Djehutymose and his son Butehamun provides valuable information about the state of affairs in Thebes during the reign of Ramesses XI in the uncertain times at the end of the New Kingdom. As a trusted aide of the generals in charge of Upper Egypt Djehutymose had to travel to Nubia and places within Egypt to report on events there while Butehamun kept management of affairs at Thebes. The letter below from Year 10 of the Renaissance Period opens with wishes for the blessings of the Theban gods on the General Piankh. There is a report on the receipt and reading of the general's last letter, then a report on the fact that the Theban contigent was too slow in sending some clothes for Piankh and that his wife suggested Djehutymose deliver them in person to Piankh in Nubia. This domestic-sounding detail actually reveals that Piankh was extremely busy with threatening events in Nubia. The letter concludes with some difficulties over a building commission and the progress of the search for an ancient tomb in the necropolis. The standard greeting

15. Hieratic letter of the scribe Butehamun, written from right to left (P. British Museum, EA 10375). The signs are relatively large for the greeting at the beginning, then become smaller so that they fit on this sheet of papyrus.

formulae, such as 'may Amun bring you back safe and you fill your embrace with Ne (Thebes) and we fill our eyes with the sight of you when you have returned alive, prospering and healthy', are combined with evocative descriptions such as that of Djehutymose just missing Piankh: 'He just about died when we reached Ne and he was told you had gone before we had reached our mistress!'[1]

Hieratic documents

The range of hieratic documents is enormous, covering every type of document that could be written, including administrative tax accounts, day books recording the workers in the Valley of the Kings and their days off, formal state court records and the attendant investigation reports, land leases, and wills. There are also literary works and stories, poems, hymns, and prayers, dream interpreters' guides, magical spells, medical texts, and books of literary teachings and etiquette (inadequately called Wisdom Texts). There are temple inventories, records of the rituals to be carried out in the temple, the books of knowledge of the temple, the *Book of That which is in the Underworld* (guide book for the afterlife), and other books dealing with the next life. There are letters between individuals, letters to the dead, official letters asking for supplies to be sent to a royal work party, and more treasured letters. One letter written by King Pepi II to an individual called Harkhuf asked him to look after a pygmy he was bringing to the king as a gift. The letter was so valued that Harkhuf had a hieroglyphic version of it inscribed onto his tomb entrance at Aswan. There are surviving receipts and accounts by the million for everything from donkeys to lists of laundry. The modern propensity for the written word is not new. Consider a modern dustbin or recycling bin and its contents from letters to council circulars, shop receipts, written packaging, leaflets, magazines— their ancient equivalent does exist, but in rarefied circumstances and in particular conditions.

Masses of these documents come from the village of the workmen who built the tombs of the kings at the Valley of the Kings in

Thebes. The inhabitants of the village of Deir el-Medina were very literate by Ancient Egyptian standards. As many of those who lived and worked there had the job of writing and carving hieroglyphs in the tombs and as many were scribes by profession, perhaps to cope with the administrative demands of such a rarefied place, there was an unusually large number of literate people in the village. Their receipts and notes ended up as infill for a huge pit excavated in the New Kingdom and to provide water. The discovery of this pit was like finding a landfill rubbish dump and sifting through the minutiae of a dustbin to piece together bits of individual lives. The texts survive on flakes of limestone and on fragments of pottery called ostraka (singular ostrakon). Some of these are hand-sized notelets that would have been placed in the palm of the hand of the scribe, fitting there snugly as they were written out. A scribe called Qenherkhopshef is recognizable by his handwriting, great sprawling hieratic signs, and by the fact that he bashed the edges of his ostraka so that they were blunted and splinters did not break off, taking part of an important note with them. He and his family also had a library containing a varied collection of papyrus books of many different kinds, presumably for their own amusement and perhaps to read out to other villagers. From this library came over 40 texts including a copy in Qenherkhopshef's hand of the 'Battle of Qadesh', the 'Story of Horus and Seth' (a kind of mythological soap opera), 'The Tale of the Blinding of Truth', 'Love Songs', 'Extracts from the Maxims of Any', hymns, recipes against greying hair and baldness, a dream book, official and private letters, and the wills and testaments of Naunakhte.[2]

Perhaps more than anything else, the material from the village hints at a vast oral and aural literary tradition of which only a tiny proportion has been preserved. Some of the stories from Egypt are only preserved in a single text such as the earlier Tales of Wonder in Papyrus Westcar, and this too seems to be a story cycle with various episodes which was committed to papyrus by a scribe at one time. The Demotic cycle of 'The Story of Petiese, son of Petetum and 70 Other Good and Bad Stories' begins with the words, 'The voice which is before Pharaoh', implying that the stories were intended to be read out before an audience.[3]

The Letters of Hekanakht were written in the early years of Senwosret I in Dynasty 12 on behalf of the *ka*-priest Hekanakht. One of his jobs was to look after the funerary cult of a vizier of Montuhotep II, called Ipi. This meant taking care of an area of land which would be cultivated to provide both the offerings for the cult and the payment in kind for Hekanakht. This man clearly had other irons in the fire, though, and his business interests sometimes took him away from home. At times like this, he sent back a stream of letters to his deputy and eldest son, Merisu, to make sure his household and his interests were being looked after. It seems likely that though he did write some of the letters by himself he also dictated others to a scribe, either because he was too busy to sit down and write them or because he had never had formal training or because his status allowed him to have a secretary. The style is very colloquial and, even in translation, he can be imagined pacing up and down, barking out thoughts and random sentences to the scribe trying to keep up with him. At one moment he is concerned that people are working hard for him; at another that everyone in his household is getting their fair rations; and then he is worried that his concubine is not being treated well by his sons and daughters. So vivid were his outpourings that Agatha Christie used them as the basis of a murder mystery set in Ancient Egypt (*Death Comes as the End*). This man's thoughts and feelings were preserved by a diligent scribe in hieratic for us to read and to enable us to look in on his life. The letters are not always very clear because only one side of the correspondence has survived, but they give much incidental information about the makeup of his household and his dependants and servants, including grown-up and young children, a widowed or unmarried sister, and a second, younger, wife who is the source of friction in the household. One of the letters was addressed to a neighbour and was found unopened, never having been forwarded by Merisu.[4]

The scribal profession

Scribes were an important part of every businessman's entourage. Important facts and figures could not be left to the memory like tales, but a good secretary taking copious notes must have given a sense of security in the face of the administration to people like Hekanakht. The line of scribes in the Tomb of Horemhab are shown wearing their elegant wigs and gowns, each one's long graceful fingers holding a pen poised above a papyrus. Their almost effete attitude contrasts uncomfortably with the African slave being punched in the face as he is dragged forward to be counted and become a statistic in an account of slaves. The four scribes shown here are presumably recording the accounts in quadruplicate.

There is no doubt, however, that scribes prided themselves on their skill and their ability. In a fictional literary teaching, a pompous scribe called Hori scolds a colleague and exhorts him to acquire the skills to organize the excavation of a lake and the building of a

16. Scribes from the Tomb of Horemhab, Saqqara, Dynasty 18.

brick ramp, to establish the number of men needed to transport an obelisk and to arrange the provisioning of a military mission. He is expected to acquire a knowledge of Asiatic geography.[5] A series of texts written by scribes for scribes and called the 'Satire of the Trades' poked fun at a variety of manual workmen, including the potter, the fisherman, the laundry man, and the soldier doing service overseas far from home. The sections end with the exhortation, 'Be a Scribe', and it is clear that the virtues of clean living, wearing fine linen, and living a rarefied, easier life were much to be admired.

The tenor of the Satire is that the scribal trade is the best and is the way to get on in life. It is assumed that everyone who wanted some sort of administrative post in one of the main divisions of the state bureaucracy essentially started learning to read and write together. Literacy was essential for all élite offices for men. Most elder sons followed in their father's footsteps, but there were also people who had risen through the ranks and sent their sons to school in order to ensure their status. How many people of natural ability were harvested along the way and given a scribal training is not known. After initial training in hieratic, men were selected to serve in one particular branch of administration. They worked as accountants in the financial institutions of state or as legal clerks in the legal administration. In temples, scribes could be priests, copying out sacred texts or performing the rituals there, or they may have had administrative duties in running the temple estates and storehouses. The army had many military scribes, keeping daily records of campaigns and accounts of supplies to the expeditionary forces. At court, scribes were responsible for everything from liaising between various departments to the construction of the king's pyramid, from negotiating a bride price for a foreign princess to setting the quotas of linen to be produced in the 'harim' institution. Each of these areas has a strong bias towards accounting and record-keeping, but each also has a specialist side. This meant that scribes were interchangeable (having transferable skills) and could move through the bureaucracy. It is no accident that some of the most powerful men in Egypt, such as the vizier, Paser, the general, Horemhab, and the priest, Herihor, had served in several offices and could convert their experience of how the state worked into royal power.

The initial training for scribes began in boyhood. Those chosen were lined up in rows, sitting with their texts on their kilts, and they chanted texts learned by heart until they could fit together hieroglyphs, words, and grammatical constructions and then read whole texts. In the New Kingdom they also copied out older, classic, set texts, including the Story of Sinuhe, which was evidently about what it was to be Egyptian, but more popular were the 'Satire of the Trades', 'Instruction of Amenemhet I', and 'Kemyt' (a compendium of model letters).[6] All texts serve the dual purpose of teaching the mechanics of reading and writing, as well as inculcating proper behaviour within the scribal and administrative profession and setting out the code of ethics for scribes. Trainee scribes who did not work hard enough were beaten on the back and those who drank too much beer and visited whorehouses were not considered to be good examples of the profession.

It is likely that all scribes learned hieratic, but only those who became draughtsmen or priests learned hieroglyphs. The recognizable training texts which have survived are mostly in hieratic and clearly this was the most useful script to learn. Very few learning aids such as dictionaries have survived from Egypt, perhaps because of over use, but some word lists and an occasional grammatical paradigm do exist. The Tanis Sign Papyrus has columns for: a hieroglyph, the hieratic equivalent, then a brief note in hieratic of what the sign is; for example, ⌒ is described as 'mouth of a human being'. The Geographical Papyrus also found in a charred mass in a house at Tanis has information in hieroglyphs about each administrative area of Egypt (nome): the name of a nome capital, its sacred barque, its sacred tree, its cemetery, the date of its festival, the names of forbidden objects, the local god, land, and lake of the city. This interesting codification of data, probably made by a priest, is paralleled by very similar editions of data on the temple walls at Edfu, for example.[7]

The arrangements of the word lists ('Onomastica') are interesting because they suggest the way in which the Egyptians thought about their language and also their world. The Onomasticon of Amenemope is divided into sections of groups of words which refer to the same idea: words for sky, water, and earth; administrative titles and occupations; classes, tribes, and types of human beings; towns of Egypt; buildings and types of land; agricultural land, cereals, and products; beverages and parts of cattle and cuts of meat. If these were used as teaching aids for spelling or for administrative and tax reference, the 'standard' terms would then have been consistently used by scribes throughout Egypt and seem to reflect the usual pragmatic approach of the Egyptians. The New Kingdom examples of such texts seem very clumsy, though, as the words are simply written in horizontal lines following one from another, collecting all the information together in one place. It must have been difficult to find the word you needed. It seems that by this time the texts were being copied and perhaps were intended as back-up copies, with scribes memorizing appropriate chunks. The Middle Kingdom Ramesseum Onomasticon is much more useful as it is set out in columns and each entry can be clearly seen. It contains, for example, a list of cattle markings showing the particular sign which was to be used for a particular type of bull:

'the wadj-sign : it is a red-bull'.[8]

The surviving medical texts have a similar function. They contain a description of the problem, the diagnosis of the disease or injury, and a prognosis and prescription. They sometimes also back up the practical advice with magical spells against evils and on behalf of the sick person. These texts have been described as 'magic' based on superstition, but they may have had a valuable psychosomatic effect, in much the same way as modern placebo medicines. The Rhind Mathematical Papyrus is an exemplary set of mathematical exercises, giving various problems, such as calculating the volume of a cylindrical grain store or the slope of a ramp – essential knowledge in pyramid-building – and then working through them, so that a scribe can follow all the steps of the process and practise it himself. The calculations required the manipulation of fractions which demonstrate a love of numbers for their own sake, but nonetheless with very practical applications.[9]

There are scribes who were recognized for their skill and wisdom while still alive as well as some even venerated after their death. A man named Bakhenkhons, who lived during the reign of Ramesses II, left behind a summary of his life on a statue dedicated in the Temple of Amun at Karnak. He had been the First Priest of Amun and a town governor, but on his statue he addresses us directly: 'I shall have you know what my achievement was when I was upon earth and every rank which I held since my birth: I spent 4 years as an excellent youngster, I spent 11 years as a youth when I was the chief of the training stables of King Menmaatre. I spent 4 years as a waab-priest of Amun, 12 years as the "God's Father of Amun", 15 years as the Third Priest of Amun, 12 years as the Second Priest of Amun and then 27 years as the First Priest of Amun.' Here is a man who reached the pinnacle of his career as the Overseer of the Priests of All the Gods and First Priest of Amun, and lived to a very old age (even if the offices ran consecutively). The clue to how he started in this profession is given in a second statue also dedicated at Karnak. Here he declares himself to be a man of Thebes and son of a Second Priest of Amun in Luxor: 'I came out of the Chamber of Writings/Scrolls as an "excellent commoner" in the Temple of the Lady of Heaven. I learnt to be a priest in the House of Amun as a son guided by his father.' This text then shows the young Bakhenkhons with an advantage at birth and going to the scribal school before following his chosen profession in the priesthood from the most lowly post upwards. The text is rather formulaic but it gives Bakhenkhons some extra titles: 'Chief of Secrets in Heaven, Earth and the Underworld; Great Seer of the Sun in Thebes; Great Sem-Priest; Supervisor of the Crafts of Ptah'.[10]

The scribe Amunhotep, son of Hapu, was even more successful. He had been a scribe and chief of priests in his home town of Athribis during the reign of Thutmose III, but in his early fifties was called to Thebes to be chief architect to Amunhotep III and to organize his massive mortuary complex and palace on the west bank. He has been described as the 'Minister for Culture' but he called himself 'the real first scribe of the king'. Around ten statues of Amunhotep were dedicated by him in different temples at Thebes. They show him with layers of flesh on his abdomen, indicating prosperity and advanced years, and a distinctive individual face. He is usually seated in scribal pose, slightly crouched over, reading the text on his lap. If one is inclined to help him with a particularly difficult piece of text or hieratic handwriting, it is possible to stand behind him and read with him. The texts contain his name and titles and extol his virtues, which seem to be considerable. In addition, he offers to act as intermediary for ordinary people. If people came and poured a libation for the old scribe he offered to transmit the prayers to the god Amun himself. In fact, this might actually explain his real importance in life. In order to get to King Amunhotep, petitioners, advisers, and his generals had first to go through the scribe Amunhotep. He would know everyone, everything about everyone, including all the king's business. Amunhotep was the ideal scribe, a man who was apparently quiet and unassuming, who did not shout and brag, but was self-controlled and quiet. He commanded respect by the wisdom of his advice. At least in scribal terms, this is how he achieved this ideal pinnacle. In real life, in the cut-throat politicking of the Amunhotep court, he presumably had luck as well as other non-scribal powers and skills. So great was his reputation that he was venerated in western Thebes as wise man and local saint. A small temple was built and partly dedicated to him at Deir el Medina in the Ptolemaic period as his cult was continued for almost a thousand years.

The temple at Deir el-Medina is dedicated to a second 'saint', and also a scribe, the legendary Imhotep. He was architect to King Netjerykhet (Djoser) and responsible for the building of the Step

Pyramid, the first monumental stone structure. Little is known of him from his lifetime apart from his titles, which seem to have been 'Seal-Bearer of the King of Lower Egypt, Great Seer of the Great-Mansion, Chief of Sculptors and Masons'. For his connection with the remarkable and innovative building, he was later regarded as a scribal saint who could intercede between men and gods. Bronze statuettes of him were dedicated in temples at Saqqara and in a few other places temple shrines were also dedicated to him. He is shown seated on a block chair, wearing a cap over his shaven head and with his papyrus book unrolled on his lap. Though his memory was ancient even for the Egyptians of the New Kingdom and beyond, his profession and his success as a wise man are perhaps the real attributes which were being celebrated. It seems that such people could communicate with the gods because of their wisdom, their ability to read hieroglyphs, and their beatified status.[11]

Kings too were taught to write, and in the Middle Kingdom 'Prophecy of Neferti' King Snoferu asks for a palette and papyrus roll to record in his own hand the words about what will happen in the future, spoken by the lector-priest Neferti. In the divine realm, the ibis-headed god Thoth was the divine scribe who recorded the events of the life of the king on the leaves of the divine persea tree and accounted for the years of the king's reign by notching a palm-leaf rib as each year passed. In his baboon form he is shown wrapped around the head of human scribes, imparting intelligence, doubtless somewhat uncomfortably. The importance of scribes even extended to the afterlife, where Thoth was on hand to record the outcome of the weighing of the deceased's heart after death. Standing before Osiris, the ruler of the afterworld, the heart of the deceased was weighed on scales against the feather of *maat*. If the scales balanced or were light the person was adjudged to be 'true of voice' and proceeded to the next life. If the scales sank down, then the heart was gobbled up by a monster and the person ceased to exist. The whole proceeding was recorded in writing, like any judicial process. It was the writing which ensured existence, whether you could read it or not.

Chapter 6
The decipherment
of Egyptian

The journey towards the decipherment of Egyptian hieroglyphs began almost as soon as they had been forgotten. The latest dated hieroglyphic inscription is from the temple of Philae and the reign of the Emperor Theodosius in AD 394. Visitors to Egypt such as the Greek writers Herodotus (fifth century BC) and Strabo (first century BC to first century AD), and Diodorus of Sicily (c.40 BC) had already referred to the hieroglyphic signs as a form of unintelligible picture writing. In the fourth century AD, a Hellenized Egyptian called Horapollo made a survey of Egyptian writing and published a list of nearly two hundred signs, with his interpretation of their meaning, in *Hieroglyphica*. This work itself was lost or forgotten and the impetus to decipher hieroglyphs was lost until 1415, when a manuscript of *Hieroglyphica* was acquired on the island of Andros by Cristoforo Bundelmonti and provided the basis for the Renaissance interpretation of hieroglyphs. According to Horapollo, each sign had a symbolic meaning: the sky dropping dew meant 'education', the forequarters of a lion meant 'strength', and an owl represented foreknowledge of an abundant wine vintage. No allowance was made for a phonetic system of signs and some rather fanciful reasons for the meanings were suggested. For example, a vulture sign meant 'mother', because only female vultures were thought to exist, able to reproduce without the aid of males. In Egyptian, the vulture sign can mean 'mother', but the reason is because the phonetic pronunciation of the sign of the vulture *mwt* is the same as the word for mother. Further, the signs were supposed to have allegorical meaning based on stories and philosophy and it was thought that they held the key to hidden ancient mysteries.[1]

The first step in regaining the meaning of hieroglyphs was made by the Jesuit, Athanasius Kircher, in his book *Oedipus Aegyptiacus* (*c.*1650). He was a professor of mathematics in Rome and was interested in science and languages. He studied Coptic manuscripts brought to Europe, compiled a Coptic grammar, and recognized for the first time that Coptic was a direct descendant of Ancient Egyptian. He, too, was side-tracked, however, and translated hieroglyphic texts based on symbolic inferences.

In 1799 part of a temple stela was discovered by the French scholars of Napoleon in Rosetta. The Rosetta Stone contains a priestly decree in honour of Ptolemy V which was set up in a major temple, perhaps at Saïs, in 196 BC. The surviving fragment of granite is inscribed with the decree to guarantee lands and endowments to the temples of Egypt, but crucially it has the same text in three languages: Egyptian hieroglyphs, Egyptian Demotic, and Greek. The importance of the stone for the possible decipherment of hieroglyphs was recognized straight away and attempts began almost at once to work on the script. Even though the Rosetta Stone was handed over to the British as part of the spoils of the Napoleonic War, the texts had by then been copied and were later sent all over the world. The process of decipherment required several stages as each of the principles behind the script was discovered. With hindsight, it seems as if it were a step-by-step progression, but in fact often one person (such as Kircher) would have a good idea, but would continue to use other incorrect assumptions at the same time. So, the final triumph came from deciding which of the many permutations were correct, as in any kind of code-breaking.

17. The Canopus Decree of 238 BC. A complete stela with the same text in three languages. The Rosetta Stone may have looked like this when first set up. Cairo Museum 22816.

Some progress had already been made. First, Joseph de Guignes (1721–1800), a French orientalist and sinologist, had recognized that groups of signs had determinatives and that cartouches contained royal names. Then Georg Zoega (1755–1809), a Danish scholar, suggested that hieroglyphs could be the letters of an alphabet and also independently suggested that cartouches contained royal names. He had learnt Coptic as he felt that it would assist in his work, but his main interest was in Egyptian obelisks. Johan David Åkerblad (1763–1819), a Swedish diplomat, made good progress by comparing the Greek and Demotic texts on the Rosetta Stone and identified all the proper names which occur in both texts. He also identified the words for 'temples' and 'Greeks' and the suffix pronoun 'him' in Demotic. Remarkably he published a Demotic alphabet in 1802, but it seems that his concentration on the purely alphabetic nature of Demotic held him back. Thomas Young (1773–1829) was an English physician and physicist best remembered for his discovery of the wave-theory of light. He recognized the relationship with Coptic and first suggested that the Egyptian scripts used both alphabetic and non-alphabetic signs. He read the name of Ptolemy and two of his epithets and also read the name of Queen Berenike and recognized that it had a feminine egg and *t* ending. The man who perhaps coordinated and oversaw many of these discoveries was Antoine Silvestre de Sacy (1758–1838), Professor of Arabic at the École des Langues Orientales Vivantes at the Bibliothèque Nationale in Paris. He had first recognized and transcribed three names in Demotic but was held back by thinking of the language as written with an alphabetic script. He corresponded with and encouraged Young, but ultimately it was his own student who was to make the breakthrough.

Jean-François Champollion (1790–1832) was a child prodigy and linguist who knew Latin, Greek, Hebrew, Arabic, and most importantly, Coptic. By the time he was 16 Champollion was keeping his diary in Coptic. At this time, some Coptic priests in Egypt used the language in the Coptic liturgy, so although it had been preserved to some extent, it was still not very well known.

Champollion also studied Old Chinese, Persian, and Farsi and became a fellow of the teaching staff at the Lycée in Grenoble, aged 17. He had also obtained a copy of the Rosetta Stone.

The state of knowledge at this time was as follows: the name of the king, Ptolemaios, was known from the Greek and Demotic sections and could be compared with the cartouches around the king's name in the hieroglyphic section. Champollion had to make a guess about the direction of the writing and also an assumption that the name was to be read alphabetically, with each hieroglyph being a separate sign. Once he had decided this, he had the name of Ptolemy, giving him seven letters. (Independently, Young had arrived at the same point.)

In 1815, William J. Bankes, a friend of the Duke of Wellington, had found two obelisks at Philae. They were brought to Kingston Lacy, Dorset, in 1827. On one obelisk the shaft bore hieroglyphs but the base was written in Greek. Champollion obtained a copy and found the Ptolemy cartouche (of Ptolemy VIII). Also on the obelisk in the Greek was the name of the wife of the king, Kleopatra. Champollion located the cartouche and found that he now had confirmation of some letters and a few new ones. He also had two letters for *t*, but concluded that they were homophones (sounded the same). Thanks to Young, the two signs of a *t* and an egg had been recognized as a feminine ending, again confirming this was the name of a female ruler. In itself this would not have been enough to decipher much, but Champollion compiled a list of cartouches (and thus of signs) of the Ptolemaic and Roman period and published it as his *Lettre à M. Dacier relative à l'alphabet des hiéroglyphes phonétiques* in 1822.

This was the first breakthrough. It was a small step and by itself did not mean that every text could then be transliterated *and* translated, for as yet no grammatical rules, let alone vocabulary, had been established. Though it was a long way away from the Renaissance interpretation of hieroglyphs, Champollion, at this point, still thought that Egyptian was written symbolically. For the next step in understanding the language rather than just a few signs or being able to read royal names, Champollion used copies of texts from Abu Simbel with the cartouches of another king, thought to be the famous ruler Ramesses II, mentioned in the Bible. Champollion already had the letter-sound *s*, and so to the fox-skins he gave the value *m*. The sun disk sign seemed clear and Champollion knew that in Coptic the word for sun was *r-e*. So he read the signs as *r-e m-s sw* 'Ramesses'. Also in the cartouche was the name of another god, Amun, with the canal sign at the end of the cartouche. Champollion guessed that a king was often called beloved of a god. Again in Coptic the word for 'to love' is *me*, thus this part of the cartouche would actually mean 'beloved of Amun' and in essence the first translation, rather than just rendering the signs, had been achieved.

What Champollion had discovered was that Egyptian writing combined signs for sounds with signs for ideas and he published his results in 1824, in his *Précis du système hiéroglyphique*. Using all the tools at his disposal and treating the texts as a language, not just two scripts, Champollion continued to collect texts and work through them, dividing out the word groups and applying each new piece of information as he found it. Though not everyone accepted his discovery at first, the study of Egyptian was spurred on by the Champollion breakthrough. With the recognition of different function for signs, the text on the Rosetta Stone could be divided up into words. The meaning of some words could be guessed by comparison with the Greek text and Coptic words. The grammar of the text could be studied by comparison with Coptic, though there was still some way to go.

Egyptian language studies

Various scholars studied the language, forming themselves into distinct 'schools' in Egyptology, but the first major publication after Champollion was a grammar of Demotic by Heinrich Brugsch in 1855. Brugsch was already a major figure in early Egyptology when he first noted the Semitic side to Egyptian grammar and then collected the information in a more systematic way. His *Dictionnaire hiéroglyphique et démotique*, the first systematic dictionary for hieroglyphs, was published in seven volumes between 1867 and 1882 and consisted of 3,146 pages. Adolphe Erman (1854–1937), Professor of Egyptology at the University of Berlin, was the first to recognize the different stages of the Egyptian language, but his greatest work after his *Neuägyptische Grammatik* (1880) and *Ägyptische Grammatick* (1894) was the *Wörterbuch* (dictionary) project. Based in Berlin, a team of twenty scholars went through all known Egyptian texts from Egypt and in museums and made paper slips for every word. These *Zettel* comprised the writing of the word in hieroglyphs, its transliteration, translation, and where the word occurred. They were then filed and organized so that the spellings and range of use for all known words could be established. The *Wörterbuch*, co-edited by Hermann Grapow, appeared in five volumes from 1926 to 1931 and it is still a standard reference dictionary for Egyptian. It is now available on the Internet and continues the work of collecting texts and their analysis. Another German philologist from the 'Berlin School', Kurt Sethe, made important discoveries in Egyptian grammar, re-edited and collated the Pyramid Texts and copied historical texts, which were published as *Urkunden der 18. Dynastie* from 1906 to 1909.

The fundamentally important effort was in the copying, collection, and publication of textual material in order to make it available to as many people as possible. Smaller texts from the backs of statues, for example, were published in the German *Zeitschrift für Ägyptische Sprache* (from 1863) and the French *Recueil de travaux relatifs à la philologie et à l'archéologie égyptiennes et assyriennes* (from 1889), while a concerted effort was made by scholars to make available larger bodies of material, such as complete sets of temple inscriptions. Emmanuel de Rougé and Émile Chassinat pioneered the publication of the texts in the Ptolemaic temples of Edfu and Dendera by the French Institute. The work continued with the publication of the Coffin Texts, material from Deir el Medina and the collection of all texts from the Ramesside period by Kenneth

Kitchen. In all cases, the scholars concerned have been able to make the texts available not just as a source but also in translation. The work on the monuments has been paralleled by publication of papyri and ostraka by scholars such as Alan Gardiner, Georges Posener, and Jaroslav Černý. The hieratic material was first put out in facsimile photographs so that mistakes would not be made in copying the handwriting. Many of the large-scale publications were prohibitively expensive and obtainable only by specialist libraries, by subscription, or by scholars with private means.

It is perhaps no accident that it was one such English scholar, (Sir) Alan Gardiner (1879–1963), who published the influential *Egyptian Grammar* in 1927. He was an eminent Egyptologist who had been one of the Berlin Dictionary team and he concentrated on the publication of tombs and hieratic papyri and ostraka. His *Grammar* was written very much along the traditional lines of a classical grammar book and the way in which the grammar book was constructed meant that it could be used as a didactic volume, the format of which has had enormous impact on the teaching of Egyptian.

The book is divided into sections dealing with specific grammatical issues. These are explained, exemplified from real texts, and then at the end of the section there is an exercise for the student in which they can practise what they have learnt. At various points along the way there is an 'Excursus', which deals with some aspect of Egyptian culture, such as 'Weights and Measurements', 'Time Keeping', and 'Kings' Names'. At the end of the book is a list of all the signs for Middle Egyptian, with an explanation of what each sign depicts and its use and meaning. The Gardiner Sign-List has been extremely influential in its classification of individual hieroglyphs and this section of the grammar has never really been bettered. There then follows an English to Egyptian and Egyptian to English vocabulary list. The reason for this is that, as in classical studies, it was not enough to translate *from* the language; one needed to be able to go back from English into Egyptian. Of course, this is a very artificial procedure, but it was designed to enable students to write their own hieroglyphs and to think like Egyptians.

Many other grammar books have appeared in order to address other stages of the language such as Late Egyptian, Demotic, Coptic, and Old Egyptian, and in 1924 the earliest grammar of Ancient Egyptian in Arabic was published by Antoine Zikri. Gardiner's work was so magisterial and so relatively cheap, as it was subsidized by the Oxford Griffith Institute, that it continued to be the standard grammar for students of Egyptian. Developments in understanding Egyptian, however, have overtaken the book, as has the nature of people wanting to learn Egyptian hieroglyphs, and so in recent years there have been successful attempts to update Gardiner.[2]

Some of the English school curricula do not include English grammar as such, with the result that students who lack a background knowledge of grammar from another language have to study English grammar before they can tackle Gardiner. Popular courses teaching adults Egyptian have concentrated on giving students enough skills to enhance their visits to museums with Egyptian collections or on visits to Egypt. The kind of texts in most of these places will be monumental texts, sometimes with very formulaic expressions (for example the standard funerary offering formula) or with easily recognizable cartouches. Such expressions and their meaning can be easily learnt without having to worry about the sometimes complex grammar underneath. Arising out of such a teaching programme, Bill Manley and Mark Collier's *How to Read Egyptian Hieroglyphs* has been successful in persuading a very interested general public that, for £10, they really can read hieroglyphs. An individual investment in time and application is still required and local Egyptology societies can sometimes provide a focus for such study.

Recent linguistic developments have also been applied to Egyptian grammar. Scholars have been applying ideas from the field of linguistics to Ancient Egyptian, building on studies of the language over the last forty years. The use of the 'Second Tense' in Egyptian has indicated that there are subtle ways in which the written language conveys ideas about emphasis and marks out the important parts of sentences. It has long been noticed that the final consonant is doubled in certain verbs, but the reason for this was not understood until the linguist Hans Polotsky suggested that this was the forerunner of the Coptic Second Tense. This tense throws emphasis onto the adverbial part of the sentence written at the end, thus 'He went to the house' becomes 'To the house he went'.

Other aspects of Egyptian, such as the definition of exactly how verbs should be understood, have also advanced. The concept of the verb as a modified noun, with various markers, either written endings, particles, pronunciation, position in sentence, suggests that Egyptian has interesting subtleties of expression. At a conference in 1986 to discuss the then current state of grammar studies, the whole process of analysing and investigating Egyptian grammar was described as 'juggling lots of balls'. Some of these balls included syntactic, semantic, and pragmatic approaches, but most crucially there was a recognition that these areas are related and that several levels operate in the Egyptian language at the same time and interact. It seems that the key to Egyptian grammar is flexibility, but within a defined framework of reference, as was demonstrated by the range of approaches represented at the Copenhagen conference.[3]

Taking into account the modern developments, Frederick Junge's *Neuägyptische Grammatik* (1999), James Allen's *Middle Egyptian Grammar* (2000), and Rainer Hannig's *Großer Handwörterbuch Ägyptisch–Deutsch* (1995) have all helped make material accessible for all interested people, not just Egyptology scholars. A visit to a local museum can provide a few hours of interest and fun, and visits to the monuments in Egypt are more possible than they used to be, so that the hieroglyphic texts can be tackled by a wider audience of readers than ever before.

Specialist areas

Increasingly, scholars have become more specialized in the kind of work they do. Each type or genre of text can be studied in detail, including poetry, literature, religious rituals, legal documentation, economic texts, funerary texts, and letters. Each individual part of a text can be studied, ranging from the different parts of grammar, words and their meanings and writings, down to individual signs and in particular the way in which determinatives really work. These studies contribute overall to the study of the history and development of ideas in Egypt.

Lexicographers have gathered together all words to do with the same thing, such as names of medicines, plant names, foreign place names, personal names, words for cooking, baking, and grilling, words used for greeting and talking to each other. To some degree this may be an artificial construct, but it does show interesting smaller aspects of Egyptian culture which fit into the overall system.

For example, one of the words for a turtle is *št3* which derives from the verb *št3* meaning 'to hide, be hidden'. The turtle's habit of hiding in the mud at the bottom of watery pools had led to it being given this name, 'the one who is hidden'. One of the names of Seth in Ptolemaic temple texts is *Mdy* and it has been suggested that this originates in the word for the Medes and Persians who invaded Egypt in the seventh century BC. The memory of the Persian soldiers in Egypt was particularly hateful as they were considered to have no respect for the Egyptian gods. This term *Mdy* then may have had particular resonance when applied to the demonic Seth.

Specialist studies of particular bodies of material can also illumine wider issues about Egypt and the Ancient World. A number of examples of diplomatic correspondence have survived from Egypt and elsewhere. For example, at the end of diplomatic negotiations between Ramesses II and the Hittite king Hattusil III a magnificent silver plaque was sent from Hatti to Pi-Ramesses. The cuneiform text in Babylonian set out the terms for peace and after ratification it was translated into Egyptian on papyrus, inscribed in hieroglyphs in the temple at Karnak, and transferred to clay tablets in cuneiform for the Hittites. The Egyptian hieroglyphic version and a Hittite clay tablet version have in fact survived. Each preserves the same text and it is interesting to see how they differ. Both versions are business-like documents setting out the terms and conditions of the peace without much recourse to hyperbole. They strike the reader as having a succinct legalistic document at their base and it is clear that they derive from the same text, which presumably would have been agreed by the bilingual and trilingual scribes of the courts of the two kings. It seems that the Egyptians were more fascinated by the Hittite seal on the silver plaque for it showed the Storm-god embracing the Hittite king and in the Egyptian document there is a verbal description of this scene.[4]

In the same vein is the diplomatic correspondence between Amunhotep III and Akhenaten and the various rulers of the Near Eastern countries and city-states in the fourteenth century BC. Only those letters which were kept in the archives at Akhetaten, the capital city of Akhenaten, survive and they are either copies of letters sent out by the Egyptians or the letters sent by the foreign rulers to the Egyptian court. They are written mostly in cuneiform script and Babylonian language, but include Egyptian names written out phonetically and give some hint as to how they may have sounded. Akhenaten Neferkheperure comes out as 'Napkhurriya', and Meritaten (daughter of Akhenaten) as 'Mayati', with Amunhotep III Nebmaatre as 'Nibmuareya'. The word for Egypt is 'Misri-ni-we', which is close to the modern name 'Misr'. They are certainly different from the modern Anglicized spellings and conventions and give some pause for thought as to the sound of Egyptian and the precise rhythm of the language.[5]

Modern hieroglyphs in the service of Egyptian

The publication of texts had to overcome a difficult technical problem from the beginning – that of handling the hieroglyphic script. The earliest publications were engraved facsimiles of handwritten material relying on the ability of the epigrapher to both copy and reproduce a text accurately, as in the monumental works of the *Description de l'Égypte*, Champollion's *Monuments de l'Égypte et de la Nubie*, and the Prussian Expedition led by Richard Lepsius, *Denkmäler aus Aegypten und Aethiopien*. With the establishment of the serious study of Egyptology and the need for the publication of books and other material printers addressed the problem of a hieroglyphic font. Publishers used to typeset books, that is, each page was laid out using individual metal type for each word. For alphabets of twenty-odd signs this meant having thousands of similar letters per page and the technique of setting them in place was a considerable skill. For typesetting hieroglyphs the labour involved was no less, but the production of the signs was more difficult, as hundreds of different signs were used for Middle Egyptian alone. In addition, the signs could be quite complex or detailed. The French Institute in Cairo (*Institut Français d'Archéologie Orientale*, IFAO) was at the forefront of the development of a hieroglyphic font for its publication of Edfu and Dendera temples, requiring thousands of different signs. The signs had to be accurately copied from the temple walls and cut in metal typeface, then laid out to create the page and printed off. The earlier IFAO font consisted of outline signs, so that additional detail could be put in the interior of the sign if necessary. This must have been a very time-consuming process, but it was later decided that the best compromise was to have solid signs which contained the necessary fine detail for Ptolemaic hieroglyphs.[6] For the first eight volumes of Edfu Temple alone there are over three thousand printed pages full of hieroglyphs, a truly monumental work carried on today by Sylvie Cauville and her team at both Edfu and Dendera temples.

In Germany, fonts had been developed to print grammars and the

Zeitschrift für Aegyptische Sprache and the Theinhardt font comprised 'open' hieroglyphs with clear internal details (1875). In England in 1892, the publishers Harrison and Sons already had a list of fifteen different types of Egyptian Hieroglyphic Type used for British Museum publications and others. They were produced in an environment where the Society for the Promotion of Christian Knowledge (SPCK) was printing the Bible in local languages and scripts for distribution all over the world, so the production of one more script alongside Urdu, Ethiopic, Chinese, and Arabic was not a problem.

The other main font for hieroglyphs was produced by the Griffith Institute in Oxford, essentially for the production of Gardiner's *Grammar*. The design of the hieroglyphs was put out to artists who had worked in the Theban tombs, Norman and Nina de Garis Davies. Nina Davies had written a book about Egyptian hieroglyphs, reproducing the most elaborate signs in all their artistic glory in a series of watercolour facsimiles. Working with Gardiner, the two of them established a distinctive font with considerable detail in the reproduction of each sign. Their skill was matched by the unsung craftsmen working for Oxford University Press, in particular a Mr W. J. Bilton.[7] The Oxford font was specially designed to be available in Britain and only intended for short pieces of text, so that many long texts continued to be produced in handwritten facsimiles. This did provide the opportunity for gifted Egyptological palaeographers to demonstrate their skills, usually anonymously – for example Herbert Fairman with his transcriptions of Middle Egyptian stories, onomastica, and texts from Edfu Temple. The font has survived as the Cleo font, a computer font designed by Cleo Huggins and based on the font commissioned by Gardiner.

Computer-generated hieroglyphs

One of the original focuses of the Centre for Computer-Aided Egyptological Research (CCER) was the production of a new computer font for hieroglyphs and of a word-processing program so that hieroglyphic computer documents could be written. It came about as a true team effort from 1988, led by Jochen Hallof and Dirk van der Plas.[8] Eric Aubourg's original MacScribe and WinScribe has evolved into a sophisticated application, allowing texts to be written in vertical or horizontal lines, from right to left or left to right, with the ability to group signs at will and render parts of texts in red. The hieroglyphic text can also be pasted into any word-processing package, making the production of texts easy. The CCER font and word-processing application came concomitantly with other computer-glyphs, such as Saqqara Technology's Inscribe software (1994), fun learning packages, and Egyptian games on computer, such as Senet, not just computer-games with an Egyptian theme. The CCER has taken the process one step further because it offers not only a standard font-set of 700 signs, but for those who are more adventurous, a full Ptolemaic complement. This might not seem to be for the faint-hearted but it has proved to be the making of the whole enterprise. The French Institute in Cairo has been continuing the publication of the Temple of Dendera and saw the opportunity to move to computer-produced text with the CCER's program. The volumes of the Osiris Chapels are neat and clean versions of the temple texts, with 'new' signs designed as needed, both expanding and developing the font-set available. At the same time, it is possible to work at the temple wall with a laptop computer, enter the texts straight into a publishable format and also begin to make the translations. Imagine the facility of being able to check a text straight from the stone, without having to check photographs or wait to go back to the monument at a later date. The other aspect of this work is that it is possible to upload the text to a server and make it instantly available on the web. Wall to web on the same day! With a webcam, students studying a particular text could even access their text instantly in whatever museum or other location in Egypt and work from the original, adding an extra dimension to their studies. Such facilities are also important in the consideration of access to the text, legibility, visibility, and conservation of texts.

Importance of the decipherment of hieroglyphs

The achievements of philologists have opened up a rich source of information about Egypt. The discipline of Egyptology is often said to have begun with the decipherment of hieroglyphs. Textual information does fill out our knowledge of Ancient Egypt and without it our understanding of the ancient culture would be much less varied, even though statistically so little has survived. Archaeology has provided the architectural contexts, the material evidence for religious and burial practices, the specialist goods manufactured for the élite, and sometimes even the bodies of the Egyptians themselves. Textual information, however, has given us the names of those people and their jobs, their thoughts, their poetry, and the things in which they were interested, thus showing us either their wider cosmic view or the small things which worried them. These private thoughts, tax returns, the minutiae of life, and even important state events would not survive in any meaningful way in an archaeological context. For example, we would not know that Amenemhet I was assassinated if it were not for a teaching which begins with his death and continues as his spirit gives advice to his son. The court records detailing the Tomb Robbery trials give a picture of corruption and neglect in Egypt of the Late New Kingdom and suggest that the west bank at Thebes was essentially surviving on the fruits of tomb-robbing. The words of Akhenaten to his god are personal and affecting, the pleas of the Letters to the Dead speak of bereavement and love after death, the jokes of the boatmen in the papyrus swamps bring life to the past, the visit of Amun to the mother of Hatshepsut is full of implicit eroticism and joy.

For the archaeologist in Egypt there is no escape from hieroglyphs, as even in the most difficult excavations in Pharaonic contexts textual information will always be found, even if it is a simply a small ring bezel bearing a royal cartouche. The types of information from the archaeological and textual records can highlight different aspects of the life-story of a site. The city of Saïs is well known from religious texts and votive statuary of Dynasty 26. At this time, the major cult centre of the goddess Neith here was administered by a series of powerful local governors and there were temples to Atum, Osiris, Hathor, and perhaps Sobek, among others. In addition, a statue records the construction of a sacred lake with information about its exact size, there was a special place for the rearing of the Sacred Cow of Neith, and sarcophagi attest to an important necropolis area. None of these places has been located archaeologically and it is likely, in fact, that buildings such as the Neith Temple have been totally removed from the site. On the other hand, recent archaeological work has discovered that there are two major city zones at Saïs, that human occupation here goes back to the Neolithic Period (*c.*4500 BC) and that there is a substantial Late Ramesside settlement at the site. None of these things is clear from the texts. Together, however, the two types of investigation fill out the history and life of the ancient city from earliest times to the modern day. The combined evidence can supply information as diverse as the influence of the river on the city (from geoarchaeological investigation) to the presence of the collaborator Wedjahorresne at Saïs in the Persian Period (from the hieroglyphic text on his statue). For the Egyptologist with an interest in piecing together each part of the jigsaw, each nugget, whether inscribed in stone or written in the delta mud, is treasure.[9] Texts and art, the objects and monuments, work together to provide us with a picture of the past society and its people.

Chapter 7
Hieroglyphs in the
modern world

An exhibition called 'Time Machine' at the British Museum in
1994 brought together ancient and modern art, using Ancient
Egypt as the inspiration for contemporary art. An etched
zinc plate by David Hiscock showed the hieroglyphs of the Rosetta
Stone extruded to form a modern barcode, implying that they
were both linked by their common encoded information which
could be understood only if the reader had the key. The barcode
requires a computer program and a piece of hardware, whereas
the Rosetta Stone requires a knowledge of hieroglyphs to 'crack
the code'. Such is the power of the image of the Rosetta Stone that
it has come to represent the key to Egyptian hieroglyphs, despite
the fact that the hieroglyphs on it were written in the Ptolemaic
period, by which time the picture writing was remote even by
Egyptian standards.[1]

The power of the inscribed stone comes directly through to us from
Egypt, when, in the Late Period, 'magical' statues were set up in
the precincts of temples, covered in hieroglyphs which recorded
magical spells to cure scorpion and snake bites, to drive away the
terrors of the night, and to have the gods and their minions provide
protection. Water poured over the stone and hieroglyphs was
collected to be used internally or externally; a touch of the stone
could heal. It was not necessary to read the text, simply to believe in
its power. This power can be seen earlier, when kings handed out

gifts to their courtiers, such as jars of ointment to celebrate the Sed-festival of Pepi II. The alabaster vessels were inscribed with the king's name on the side, perhaps to enhance the rejuvenating power of the ointment. Oyster shells, real and made of precious metals, were handed out to courtiers of Senrosret I during the Middle Kingdom. The king's name was inscribed on them to enhance the health-giving powers of the shell, whose name in Egyptian meant 'wholeness'. During Dynasty 18, rings made from relatively cheap faience had the names of Amunhotep Nebmaatre and Akhenaten, Smenkhare, and Tutankhamun on the bezels. Small, beautifully made cosmetic jars bear the names of Tiye and Amenhotep, with the names almost acting as amuletic devices. The objects are reminders of the king and invoke his power, using the hieroglyphic script. The detail of the text was not important and the plaques put into the foundation deposit of the temple at Tell el-Balamun have such careless writings of the name of Sheshonq III and such abbreviated titles for the priest, Hor, that they can hardly be read.[2]

Sometimes hieroglyphs are used for symbolic decoration: walls have framing borders of *ankh*-signs, *was*-sceptres, and *djed*-signs bringing 'life, power, stability'; a cartouche-shaped box of Tutankhamun has his name inlaid on the lid. Further, all Egyptian amulets could be regarded as hieroglyphs, spelling out the names of the powers they invoke.

Nevertheless, the most accessible texts were those written in hieratic, not hieroglyphs, and it may be the lack of the 'power-decoration' in the hieratic script that accounts for the retention of the hieroglyphic script. Even in modern times, we have retained the original use to which hieroglyphs were put and turned them into decorative features, so that we can write our own names, print them onto T-shirts and use their visual qualities. Even scholars have indulged in this game of paradox, however, because in modern studies hieratic originals are usually transcribed into hieroglyphs to be studied by students. It would be much easier for people to learn hieratic from the start, as this would provide a wide range of texts, relating to a wider social group, than texts written in hieroglyphs. After all, Chinese characters are learnt successfully by millions of people, so there is no reason why hieratic and Demotic should be considered difficult. The script of hieratic was somewhat neglected from the palaeographical study of Georg Möller in 1909–12 (*Hieratische Paläographie*) to the new version by Ursula Verhoeven, perhaps mainly due to the problems of the exact reproduction of the texts. The same problems applied to Demotic but, with the introduction of digital technology, it is now possible to make some of these texts more quickly and cheaply accessible, as has been done for the Demotic Dictionary Project, the Tebtunis (Greek) papyri at Michigan University, or the Deir el-Medina hieratic ostraka. They can be viewed on the web and so are instantly accessible to anyone with access to the Internet.[3]

Hieroglyphs in translation

In the modern world, the communication of Egyptian texts to us is made possible in many ways, based on the platform of scholarship of the last two hundred years. There have been great strides in translating Egyptian texts into modern languages, though this has brought another range of choices of communication. The natural inclination in translation is to transpose into a meaningful modern phrase while maintaining a balance with the original ancient text. This can result in either a complete paraphrase or an extremely stilted, literal translation which is difficult to understand. The skill in translation is finding a balance, so that the Egyptian rhythm and sentence structure can be maintained, while the sense can also be readily understood. Fashions in English language have also changed, but some forms of English seem more appropriate to some of the Egyptian material than others, in particular 'Authorized Version' English – that is, the English of the King James version of the Bible from 1611. The group of scholars who translated the Bible at this time built on other earlier attempts, in particular Tyndale's translation of the New Testament (1526) and the Pentateuch (1530).

They removed anachronisms such as the 'breeches' of Adam and Eve from the Geneva or 'Breeches' Bible of 1560 and retained the poetry and drama of the texts.[4] Egyptian translations have also gone through this process of refinement, but as many hieroglyphic texts are already 'archaic', more archaic language in translation seems justified. There are controversial areas of understanding, particularly in 'historical' matters or often at key moments of a tale, but every person who comes to an Egyptian text will bring to it something of their own experience and will ultimately understand something specific to them from it. Perhaps the greater their experience of Ancient Egypt, the more accurate is their translation, just as for any foreign culture and language. As was the case for the early decipherers, permutations which get to the nub of a text only become apparent after a time.

Below are just four examples of translations of the same Hymn to the Aten from the tomb of Ay at Tell el-Amarna (*c.*1330 BC). They demonstrate the possible variations in flavour, but, interestingly, all of them respond to the poetical nature of the text.

Splendid you rise in heaven's lightland,
O living Aten, creator of life!
When you have dawned in eastern lightland,
You fill every land with your beauty.[5]

Miriam Lichtheim, 1976

You rise in perfection on the horizon of the sky,
living Aten, who started life.
Whenever you are risen upon the eastern horizon
you fill every land with your perfection.[6]

W. K. Simpson, 1972

Thou arisest fair in the horizon of Heaven, O Living Aten,
Beginner of Life. When thou dawnest in the East, thou fillest
every land with thy beauty.[7]

Cyril Aldred, 1991

Let your holy Light shine from the height of heaven,

O living Aten,

source of all life!

From eastern horizon risen and streaming,

you have flooded the world with your beauty.[8]

John L. Foster, 1998

The continued academic study and analysis of texts, not just to provide translations like those above, will continue to advance the scientific knowledge of Egyptian and the detailed knowledge of aspects of the civilization.

Learning Egyptian hieroglyphs

Interest in Ancient Egypt in our own time has sparked a need and desire to learn the ancient language and for people to be able to read the texts for themselves. Through the medium of television, the availability of comparatively cheap travel to Egypt, educational courses at all levels, and a plethora of books about the subject of Egypt, the past is accessible in a way in which it never has been before. To some extent, anyone can now easily find the means to write their name in hieroglyphs informally or, with a little more effort, find an evening class, a teaching book, or even a web-page to help them develop the language skills a little further. Some people are more focused and organized and in Britain, for example, there are local groups of like-minded people who meet regularly and arrange talks and lectures. Some people attend reading groups to read hieroglyphs for fun and because they want to know what the Egyptians wrote about. It is probably true that more people in the world today have a smattering of Egyptian hieroglyphs than was the case at any one point in Egyptian history. More present-day people have visited some of the most sacred places in Egypt than ever could or did in Ancient Egypt. Hieroglyphs are a globally recognized symbol for Ancient Egypt and with the promise of a space probe being named in hieroglyphs, who can guess how far they will permeate universal consciousness?

Of course, this cannot happen without the momentum of texts to read and these are less readily available than teaching aids. In addition, texts with good translations also need to be made available so that beginners can see where they might be going and have guidance along the way. In this respect, the publication of material on the web and on CD-ROM is ideal as it suits the pictorial nature of the script much better than other conventional methods of publication. In fact, the ability of the web and of computers to reproduce hieroglyphs easily and cheaply is almost the technical revolution for which hieroglyphs have been waiting. A text only needs to be compiled once and then it is available a million times. To this end, several institutions have been working on the publication of material. Museums have started to use the web as a means of providing access, both to the displayed collections and their reserve material. The high-quality photographs of inscribed objects can be used as ready-made learning material. Even though the availability of whole collections on the web is a long way off, simply because of the actual working hours needed to put all the information together, a good corpus is already available from the Louvre, the Cairo Museum, the Metropolitan Museum and the Petrie Museum, to name only a few. In addition, the European Union-funded Champollion Project opened up Egyptian resources by putting 15,000 objects from European museums onto CD-ROM, including photographs of objects, catalogue data, and hieroglyphic texts. The eventual home of projects like this is in cyberspace. This will allow researchers on the web to have access to the material and some of them will have contributions to make to cataloguing or understanding the objects.

More complex than this basic copying of texts has been the work pioneered by Peter Der Manuelian in computer digital epigraphy. The facsimile copying of tomb and temple wall scenes has largely been done by hand for the last 150 years, either by the use of photographs or working directly from the wall, sometimes onto paper or plastic. The results have been spectacular, particularly in the work of Norman and Nina de Garis Davies in the Theban

Tombs, Amice Calverley and Myrtle Broome at Abydos, and the Chicago House Epigraphy Project at Medinet Habu. The publications were, however, expensive and difficult to reproduce cost-effectively. Peter Der Manuelian has been able to copy tomb scenes and all their texts by scanning good photographs into a drawing application and then drawing in the lines of the carving or painting. The technique requires an enormous amount of skill and expert judgement, but once the result has been fine-tuned it can be repeated *ad infinitum*, stored or made electronically accessible at will.[9] In addition, the computer-based format is more versatile in that the walls of a building can be joined together in a virtual environment so that the visitor to the tomb can move around it and have an impression of the scenes and texts in the context of the original setting. If this is the aim, there are already virtual-reality reconstructions of the Tomb of Nofretari and the Temple of Abu Simbel.[10]

Modern hieroglyphs and Egyptian

With the prospect of Ancient Egyptian hieroglyphs being scanned directly from original location to personal computer, will all the available texts be read one day? At the moment this seems to be a long way off, but it may be a more attainable goal than could have been imagined even twenty years ago. In the event that scholars might run out of texts to study, modern writers of hieroglyphs could start to create new texts. Fakers of antiquities have already been doing this for a couple of hundred years, but sometimes these objects have texts copied from other objects, completely invented texts, or very poor pastiches. An inscribed object would have brought a better price on the market, so in some cases uninscribed but authentic objects were 'enhanced' with a text. Bearing in mind the possibility that the Egyptians could sometimes have been less than careful about the copying of texts, an ushabti in Cleveland Museum does have other factors going against it. In this case the text on the front of the ushabti is a *ḏd mdw in Wsir* . . . 'Words spoken by Osiris . . .' formula rather than the usual 'Illuminating the Osiris . . .' formula. This in itself is known on other ushabtis but, taken together with a mixture of stylistic details indicating different dates, it is felt on balance not to be genuine. On the other hand, a stela showing a Hathor cow and her calf has a main text of three lines of terrible hieroglyphs, reading in various directions and not really making sense, though obviously based on a real text. On that basis alone, it must be a forgery – or is it just inept?[11]

Other objects could be more seriously dangerous, such as the (in)famous scarab of Nekau II, the second king of Dynasty 26. The limestone scarab itself is not particularly noteworthy, but its inscription tells of the circumnavigation of Africa by Phoenician sailors in the employ of the king. This scarab could commemorate such an event at this time and it seems to corroborate the information from the Greek historian Herodotus (*Histories* IV, 42) about this event. In this case, Herodotus seems to have come first and the scarab was carved by the Egyptologist, Urbain Bouriant, as a birthday surprise for a colleague.[12] Looking carefully at the scarab, it is the seated-man determinatives that give it away, as they are in the style of the printed versions of this sign of the modern day.

Happily other attempts to produce hieroglyphic texts are obviously not genuine, such as some of the words which issue from the mouth of Kleopatra and the Egyptians in *Asterix and Cleopatra*.[13] There are also modern attempts to hear Ancient Egyptian. Parts of Philip Glass's opera *Akhnaten* are sung in Egyptian, including a love poem, and there are attempts to have some characters speak clear Middle Egyptian, sometimes anachronistically, in various films – for example, *The Mummy's Shroud* (1967) and *Sphinx* (1980). *The Mummy* (1999) and *Stargate* (1994), in addition, made great efforts to render Egyptian accurately and credited the Egyptologist Stuart Tyson Smith for his efforts. In each case, these are genuine attempts to create something in a dead tongue for modern ears, and Ancient Egyptian hieroglyphs may turn out not to record such a dead language after all. Perhaps, then, we really will be able to think in Ancient Egyptian and begin to recreate a clear image of the past. But will it be in our image or in theirs?

Notes

Chapter 1: The origins of writing in Egypt

1 H. Winkler, *The Rock Inscriptions of Southern Upper Egypt, I–II*, London: Egypt Exploration Society, 1938–9.

2 B. Midant-Reynes, *The Prehistory of Egypt*, Oxford: Blackwell, 2000, 149–50 Gilf Kebir/Uweinat.

3 For boats on pottery, see G. P. Gilbert, 'Some Notes on Prehistoric Decorated Vessels with Boat Scenes', *The Bulletin of the Australian Centre for Egyptology*, 10, 1999, 19–37 and personal communication.

4 Tomb 100: J. E. Quibell and F. W. Green, *Hierakonpolis II*, London: Quaritch, pls. LXXV–LXXIX; dating by B. J. Kemp, *Ancient Egypt: Anatomy of a Civilization*, Cambridge University Press, 1989, 40–1.

5 Naqada IIIa2 around 3200 BC: G. Dreyer, *Umm el-Qaab I Das prädynastische Königsgrabe U-j und seine frühen Schriftzeugnisse*, Mainz am Rhein: Phillip von Zabern, 1998.

6 Den: W. M. F. Petrie, *The Royal Tombs of the First Dynasty 1900, I*, London: Egypt Exploration Fund, 1900; the re-excavation is published by G. Dreyer *et al.*, 'Nachuntersuchungen im frühzeitlichen Königsfriedhof 9/10 Vorbericht', *Mitteilungen des deutschen archäologisches Instituts in Kairo* 54, 1998, 141–64; G. Dreyer *et al.*, 'Nachuntersuchungen im frühzeitlichen Königsfriedhof 11/12 Vorbericht', *MDAIK* 56, 2000, 97–118. The seal-box is now in the British Museum, EA 35.552.

Chapter 2: Hieroglyphic script and Egyptian language

1 All fragments of the stone are conveniently published by T. A. H. Wilkinson, *Royal Annals of Ancient Egypt: The Palermo Stone and its Associated Fragments*, London and New York: Kegan Paul International, 2000.

2 Inflection is where the spelling and pronunciation of a word is changed to show different roles or uses in a sentence. It is obvious in Latin: for example in *canis latrarat* 'the dog barks' *canis* is the subject (the one who does the action), but in *canem homo calcitrat* 'the man kicks the dog', *canem* with a different spelling is now the object and suffers from the action of the subject.

3 Pseudo-verbal constructions are so called because they involve verbs which are used as if they were adverbs. The term is now a little outdated but is used in the main Egyptian grammar books.

4 J. P. Allen, *The Inflection of the Verb in the Pyramid Texts*, Malibu: Udena Publications, 1984 has useful comments on epigraphic peculiarities and the verb.

5 Meroitic Hieroglyphs after F. Ll. Griffith, *Meroitic Inscriptions, Part I: Sôba to Dangêl*: London: Egypt Exploration Fund, 1911: No. 60, pl. XXXII and pp. 82–3. Cursive Meroitic after F. Ll. Griffith, *Meroitic Inscriptions, Part II: Napata to Philae and Miscellaneous*, London: Egypt Exploration Fund, 1912: No. 85, pl. VII and pp. 13–14.

Chapter 3: Hieroglyphs and art

1 Hieroglyphs orientation: H. Fischer, 'L'inversion de l'écriture égyptienne', in *L'écriture et l'art de l'Égypte ancienne*, Paris: Presses Universitaires de France, 1986, 51–93.

2 Sabine Kubisch, 'Die Stelen der 1 Zwischenzeit aus Gebelein', *MDAIK* 56 (2000), 239–65, see Abb. 1 p. 246; Sir Arthur Conan Doyle, 'The Adventure of the Dancing Men', from *The Return of Sherlock Holmes*, London: John Murray, 1905.

Chapter 4: 'I know you, I know your names'

1 Translation from A. G. McDowell, *Village Life in Ancient Egypt*, Oxford: Oxford University Press, 1999, 118–20.

2   For a parallel version of the text see W. Murnane and C. C. Van
    Siclen III, *The Boundary Stelae of Akhenaten*, New York and
    London: Kegan Paul International, 1993, text VII:B, 95–6.

3   Originally published by J. E. Quibell, *The Ramesseum*, London:
    Egypt Exploration Fund, 1896. Contents listed by R. B. Parkinson,
    The Tale of the Eloquent Peasant, Oxford: Griffith Institute and
    Ashmolean Museum, 1991, xi–xiii.

4   British Museum no. 498, trans. M. Lichtheim, *Ancient Egyptian
    Literature, Volume I: The Old and Middle Kingdom*, Berkeley:
    University of California Press, 1973, 51–7.

5   Trans. M. Lichtheim, *Ancient Egyptian Literature, Volume III: The
    Late Period*, Berkeley: University of California Press, 1980, 125–38.

6   S. Sauneron, *Le Temple d'Esna*, Cairo: IFAO, 1963, 126. Crocodile
    readings: J.-C. Goyon, *Valeurs phonétiques des signes
    hiéroglyphiques d'époque gréco-romaine*, Montpellier: Service des
    Publications de la Recherche de l'Université de Montpellier, 1988,
    ii. 350–1.

7   J. Zandee, *An Ancient Egyptian Crossword Puzzle*, Leiden: Ex
    Oriente Lux, 1966; H. M. Stewart, 'A Crossword Hymn to Mut',
    Journal of Egyptian Archaeology, 57 (1971), 87–104; R. B.
    Parkinson, *Cracking Codes: The Rosetta Stone and Decipherment*,
    London: British Museum, 1999, 84–5.

8   Louvre C12, E. Drioton, 'Recueil de cryptographie monumentale',
    Annales du Service des Antiquités de l'Égypte, 40 (1940), 306–427.

9   Kenneth Williams as Julius Caesar, in *Carry On Cleo*, scripted by
    Talbot Rothwell and directed by Gerald Thomas, 1965.

Chapter 5: Scribes and everyday writing

1   For the transcription see J. Černý, *Late Ramesside Letters*, Brussels:
    Fondation Égyptologique Reine Élisabeth, 1939, no. 28, pp. 44–8;
    translation after E. Wente, *Letters from Ancient Egypt*, Atlanta:
    Scholars Press, 1990, 194–5.

2   Listed by A. G. McDowell, *Village Life in Ancient Egypt: Laundry
    Lists and Love Songs*, Oxford: Oxford University Press, 1999,
    134–5, based on the work of P. W. Pestman, 'Who were the Owners
    in the "Community of Workmen" of the Chester Beatty Papyri?', in

R. J. Demarée and J. J. Janssen (eds.), *Gleanings from Deir el-Medina*, Leiden: Nederlands Instituut voor het Nabije Oosten, 1982, 155–72.

3   K. Ryholt, *The Story of Petiese, son of Petetum and 70 Other Good and Bad Stories*, Copenhagen: Museum Tusculanum Press, 1999.

4   T. G. H. James, *The Letters of Hekanakhte and Other Early Middle Kingdom Documents*, New York: Metropolitan Museum of New York, 1962; see also for extracts and discussion R. B. Parkinson, *Voices from Ancient Egypt*, London: British Museum Press, 1991, 101–7.

5   P. Anastasi I, P. Koller, and A. H. Gardiner, *Egyptian Hieratic Texts: Literary Works of the New Kingdom, Part I*, Leipzig: J. C. Hinrichs, 1911; E. Wente, *Letters from Ancient Egypt*, 98–110.

6   From preserved texts Annie Gasse has put together a top six texts, but also points out that the preservation of texts is extremely uneven. A. Gasse, 'Les ostraca hiératiques de Deir el-Medina: nouvelles orientations de la publication', in R. J. Demarée and A. Egberts (eds.), *Village Voices*, Leiden: CNWS, 1992, 51–70.

7   F. Ll. Griffith and W. Petrie, *Two Hieroglyphic Papyri from Tanis*, London: Egypt Exploration Society, 1889.

8   A. H. Gardiner, *Ancient Egyptian Onomastica*, 3 vols., Oxford: Oxford University Press, 1947.

9   G. Robins and C. Shute, *The Rhind Mathematical Papyrus*, London: British Museum Press, 1998.

10 Bakhenkhons: texts Munich, Staatlicher Sammlung Ägyptische Kunst, Gl. WAF 38 and Karnak, Cairo CGC 42155 and in K. A. Kitchen, *Ramesside Inscriptions, III*, 295–9.

11 D. Wildung, *Egyptian Saints: Deification in Pharaonic Egypt*, New York: New York University Press, 1977.

Chapter 6: The decipherment of Egyptian

1   G. Boas, *The Hieroglyphics of Horapollo*, Princeton: Princeton University Press, 1993.

2   A self-survey of the state of Egyptian language studies was undertaken by Egyptologists in 1972: S. Sauneron (ed.), *Textes et langages de l'Égypte pharaonique: Cent cinquante années de*

recherches 1822–1972. Hommage à Jean-François Champollion, 2 vols., Cairo: IFAO, 1972.

3   J. Johnson, 'Focusing on Various "Themes"', in P. Frandsen and G. Englund (eds.), Crossroad: Chaos or the Beginning of a New Paradigm. Papers from the Conference on Egyptian Grammar 1986, Copenhagen: Carsten Niebuhr Institute of Ancient Near Eastern Studies, 401–10.

4   The translations by J. A. Wilson (Egyptian) and A. Goetze (Hittite) can be compared in J. Pritchard (ed.), Ancient Near Eastern Texts Relating to the Old Testament, Princeton University Press, 1950 (and later editions), 199–203; also see K. A. Kitchen, Pharaoh Triumphant, Warminster: Aris & Phillips, 1982, 75–9.

5   W. L. Moran, The Amarna Letters, Baltimore: Johns Hopkins University Press, 1992.

6   The 2002 catalogue of the Institut Français d'Archéologie Orientale shows the early typesetting process and font (p. 3).

7   A. H. Gardiner, Egyptian Grammar, 3rd edn., Oxford: Griffith Institute, 1979, ix–xvi.

8   N. Grimal, J. Hallof, and D. van der Plas, Hieroglyphica, Volume I, Utrecht and Paris: CCER, 1993 with 4,706 signs; extended list in Hieroglyphica, Volume I 2, Utrecht and Paris: CCER, 2000.

9   P. Wilson, The Survey of Saïs (forthcoming) and reports since 1997 in the Journal of Egyptian Archaeology.

Chapter 7: Hieroglyphs in the modern world

1   David Hiscock, no. 5, 'Time Machine: Ancient Egypt and Contemporary Art', British Museum and Institute of International Visual Arts, 1994.

2   A. J. Spencer, Excavations at Tell el-Balamun 1995–1998, London: British Museum Press, 1999, 90.

3   Tebtunis papyri: http://sunsite.berkeley.edu/APIS/ (current in Summer 2002); Deir el-Medina online: http://www.uni-muenchen.de/dem-online/ and go to 'login' (current in Summer 2002).

4   On the skill of Biblical translations, see G. Hammond, The Making of the English Bible, Manchester: Carcanet New Press, 1982.

5 Miriam Lichtheim, *Ancient Egyptian Literature, Volume II: The New Kingdom*, Berkeley: University of California Press, 1976, 96.

6 William Kelly Simpson (ed.), *The Literature of Ancient Egypt*, New Haven: Yale University Press, 1972, 290.

7 Cyril Aldred, *Akhenaten, King of Egypt*, London: Thames & Hudson, 1988, repr. 1991, 241.

8 John L. Foster, *Echoes of Egyptian Voices. An Anthology of Ancient Egyptian Poetry*, Norman, Oka. University of Okhlahoma Press, 1998, 5–18.

9 P. Der Manuelian, '"Digital Epigraphy" at Giza', *Egyptian Archaeology* 17 (Autumn 2000), 25–7 and *Journal of the American Research Center in Egypt* 35 (1998), 97–113.

10 Abu Simbel can be seen at http://www.ccer.nl and follow links to Abu Simbel; the tomb of Nofretari was published in *Atlas of the Ancient World* by Maris Multimedia Limited at http://www.cominf.ru/maris/ and the tomb http://www.cominf.ru/maris/aaw/aawdemo/aawdemo-htm (all current in Summer 2002).

11 Published with the rest of the Cleveland Collection by L. Berman with K. Bohac, *Catalogue of Egyptian Art, Cleveland Museum of Art*, 1999, nos. 510 and 496.

12 Republished with suspicions by W. M. F. Petrie, 'The First Circuit Round Africa, and the Supposed Record of It', *Geographical Journal*, 32 (July to Dec. 1908), 480–5. Unmasked by G. Steindorff, 'Fakes and Fates of the Egyptian Antiquities', *Journal of the Walters Art Gallery, Baltimore*, 10 (1947), 54–5; confirmed by H. de Meulenaere, *Herodotos over de 26ste Dynastie*, Leuven: Universiteit van Leuven, 1951, 62.

13 Goscinny and Uderzo, *Asterix and Cleopatra*, first published 1965.

Chronology

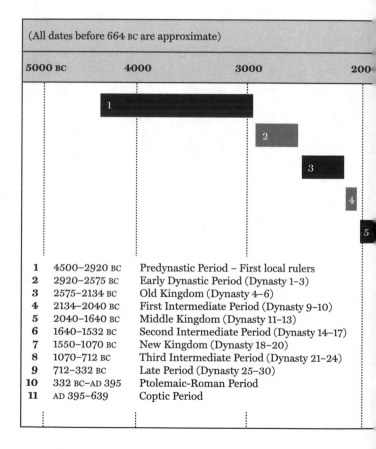

(All dates before 664 BC are approximate)

5000 BC	4000	3000	200

1	4500–2920 BC	Predynastic Period – First local rulers
2	2920–2575 BC	Early Dynastic Period (Dynasty 1–3)
3	2575–2134 BC	Old Kingdom (Dynasty 4–6)
4	2134–2040 BC	First Intermediate Period (Dynasty 9–10)
5	2040–1640 BC	Middle Kingdom (Dynasty 11–13)
6	1640–1532 BC	Second Intermediate Period (Dynasty 14–17)
7	1550–1070 BC	New Kingdom (Dynasty 18–20)
8	1070–712 BC	Third Intermediate Period (Dynasty 21–24)
9	712–332 BC	Late Period (Dynasty 25–30)
10	332 BC–AD 395	Ptolemaic-Roman Period
11	AD 395–639	Coptic Period

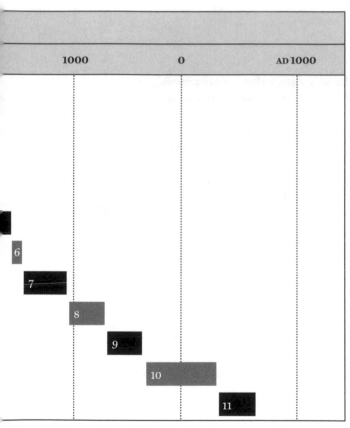

| 1000 | 0 | AD 1000 |

6

7

8

9

10

11

Further reading

The early state, writing, and its development

Baines, J., 'Literacy, Social Organization, and the Archaeological Record: The Case of Early Egypt', in J. Gledhill, B. Bender, and M. T. Larsen (eds.), *State and Society: The Emergence and Development of Social Hierarchy and Political Centralization*, London: Unwin Hyman, 1988, 192–214.

Baines, J. and Yoffee, N., 'Order, Legitimacy, and Wealth in Ancient Egypt and Mesopotamia', in G. M. Feinman and J. Marcus (eds.), *Archaic States*, Santa Fe and New Mexico: School of American Research Press, 1998, 199–260.

Parkinson, R. and Quirke, S., *Papyrus*, London: British Museum, 1995.

Postgate, N., Wang, T., and Wilkinson, T., 'The Evidence for Early Writing: Utilitarian or Ceremonial?', *Antiquity*, 69 (1995), 459–80.

The Egyptian language

Allen, J., *A Middle Egyptian Grammar*, Cambridge: Cambridge University Press, 2000.

Collier, M., and Manley, B., *How to Read Hieroglyphs*, London: British Museum Press, 1998.

Faulkner, R. O., *A Concise Dictionary of Middle Egyptian*, Oxford: Griffith Institute, 1962.

Gardiner, A. H., *Egyptian Grammar*, 3rd edn., Oxford: Griffith Institute, 1957.

Hannig, R., *Großer Handwörterbuch Ägyptisch–Deutsch*, Mainz: Phillip von Zabern, 1995.

Johnson, J. H., *Thus Wrote 'Onchsheshonqy. An Introductory Grammar of Demotic'*, 2nd edn., Chicago: Oriental Institute of the University of Chicago, 1991.

Junge, F., *Late Egyptian Grammar*, Oxford: Griffith Institute, 2001.

Loprieno, A., *Ancient Egyptian: A Linguistic Introduction*, Cambridge: Cambridge University Press, 1995.

Pestman, P., *The New Papyrological Primer*, Leiden: Brill, 1990.

Tait, W. J., 'Approaches to Demotic Lexicography', in S. P. Vleeming (ed.), *Aspects of Demotic Lexicography*, Leuven: Peeters, 1987.

Translated anthologies

Lichtheim, M., *Ancient Egyptian Literature, Volume I: The Old and Middle Kingdom*; *Volume II: The New Kingdom*; *Volume III: The Late Period*, Berkeley: University of California Press, 1973–80.

McDowell, A. G., *Village Life in Ancient Egypt*, Oxford: Oxford University Press, 1999.

Moran, W. L., *The Amarna Letters*, Baltimore: Johns Hopkins University Press, 1992.

Parkinson, R. B., *Voices from Ancient Egypt*, London: British Museum Press, 1991.

Wente, E., *Letters from Ancient Egypt*, Atlanta: Scholars Press, 1990.

Decipherment

Parkinson, R., *Cracking Codes: The Rosetta Stone and Decipherment*, London: The British Museum, 1999.

Pope, M., *The Story of Decipherment: From Egyptian Hieroglyphic to Linear B*, London: Thames & Hudson, 1975.

Index

Expand your collection of
VERY SHORT INTRODUCTIONS

Visit the
VERY SHORT
INTRODUCTIONS
Web site

www.oup.co.uk/vsi

➤ **Information** about all published titles

➤ News of **forthcoming books**

➤ **Extracts** from the books, including titles
not yet published

➤ **Reviews** and views

➤ **Links** to other **web sites** and main
OUP web page

➤ Information about **VSIs in translation**

➤ **Contact** the editors

➤ **Order** other **VSIs** on-line